Gospel Grounds and Evidences of the Faith of God's Elect

JOHN OWEN

Printed on acid free paper in the USA

British Library Cataloguing In Publication Data
A Record of this Publication is available
from the British Library

ISBN 978-1-84685-757-7

Published 2007 by
Diggory Press

Diggory Press Ltd
Three Rivers, Minions, Liskeard, Cornwall,
PL14 5LE, UK
and of Diggory Press, Inc.,
Goodyear, Arizona, 85338, USA
WWW.DIGGORYPRESS.COM

**Learn how YOU can publish your book
by visiting our website!**

Gospel Grounds and Evidences
of the Faith of God's Elect

To the Reader,

As faith is the first vital act that every true
Christian puts Forth, and the life which he lives is
by the faith of the Son of God, so it is his next
and great concern to know that he does believe,
and that believing he has eternal life; that his faith
is the faith of God's elect, and of the operation of
God: without some distinct believing knowledge
of which he cannot so comfortably assure his
heart before God concerning his calling and
election, so far as to carry him forth in all the
ways of holiness, in doing and suffering the
will of God with necessary resolution and
cheerfulness; the doing of which in a right
manner, according to the tenor of the gospel, is
no small part of spiritual skill; whereunto two
things are highly requisite: first, That he be well
acquainted with the doctrine of Christ, and know
how to distinguish the gospel from the law; and,
secondly, That he be very conversant with his
own heart, that so by comparing his faith, and the
fruits thereof, with the said doctrine of Christ, he
may come to see that, as he has received Christ,
so he walks in him: all his reasonings concerning
himself being taken up from the word of God, so
that what judgment he passes upon himself may
be a judgment of faith, and answer of a good
conscience towards God; for all the trials of faith
must at last be resolved into a judgment of faith,
before which is made, the soul still labours under
staggerings and uncertainties.

The design of this ensuing treatise is to resolve this great question, whether the faith we profess unto be true or no?—The resolution of which, upon an impartial inquiry, must needs be very grateful and advantageous to every one that has but tasted that the Lord is gracious. That the late reverend, learned, and pious Dr Owen was the author there needs be no doubt; not only because good assurance is given by such as were intrusted with his writings, but also in that the style and spirit running through the other of his practical writings is here very manifest; and, accordingly, with them is recommended to the serious perusal of every diligent inquirer into the truth of his spiritual estate and condition.

Isaac Chauncey.

Gospel Grounds and Evidences of the Faith of God's Elect;

"Examine yourselves, whether ye be in the faith; prove your own selves. Know ye not your own selves, how that Jesus Christ is in you, except ye be reprobates?"—
2 Cor.xiii. 5

Evidences of the faith of God's elect

THE securing of the spiritual comforts of believers in this life is a matter of the highest importance unto the glory of God, and their own advantage by the gospel. For God is abundantly willing that all the heirs of promise should receive strong consolation, and he has provided ways and means for the communication of it to them; and their participation of it is their principal interest in this world, and is so esteemed by them. But their effectual refreshing enjoyment of these comforts is variously opposed by the power of the remainders of sin, in conjunction with other temptations. Hence, notwithstanding their right and title unto them by the gospel, they are ofttimes actually destitute of a gracious sense of them, and, consequently, of that relief which they are suited to afford in all their duties, trials, and afflictions. Now, the root whereon all real comforts do grow, whence they spring and arise, is true and saving faith,—the faith of God's elect. Wherefore they do ordinarily answer unto, and hold proportion with, the evidences which any have of that faith in themselves; at least, they cannot be maintained without such evidences. Wherefore, that we may be a little useful unto the establishment or recovery of that consolation which God is so abundantly willing that all the heirs of promise should enjoy, I shall inquire, What are the principal acts and operations of faith, whereby it will evidence its truth and sincerity in the midst of all temptations and storms that may befall believers in this world?

And I shall insist on such alone as will bear the severest scrutiny by Scripture and experience. And,—The principal genuine acting of saving faith in us, inseparable from it, yea, essential to such acting, consists in the: choosing, embracing, and approbation of God's way of saving sinners, by the mediation of Jesus Christ, relying thereon, with a renunciation of all other ways and means pretending unto the same end of salvation.

This is that which we are to explain and prove. Saving faith is our "believing the record that God has given us of his Son," 1 John v. 10, "And this is the record, that God has given to us eternal life; and this life is in his Son," verse 11. This is the testimony which God gives, that great and sacred truth which he himself bears witness unto,—namely, that he has freely prepared eternal life for them that believe, or provided a way of salvation for them. And what God so prepares he is said to give, because of the certainty of its communication. So grace was promised and given to the elect in Christ Jesus before the world began, 2 Tim. i. 9; Tit. i. 2. And that is so to be communicated unto them, in and by the mediation of his Son Jesus Christ, that it is the only way whereby God will give eternal life unto any; which is therefore wholly in him, and by him to be obtained, and from him to be received. Upon our acquiescence in this testimony, on our approbation of this way of saving sinners, or our refusal of it, our eternal safety or ruin does absolutely depend. And it is reasonable that it should be so: for, in our receiving of this testimony of God, we "set to our seal that God is true," John iii. 33; we ascribe unto him the glory of his truth, and therein of all the other holy properties of his nature,—the most eminent duty whereof we are capable in this world; and by a refusal of it, what lies in us, we make him a liar, as in this place, 1 John v. 10, which is virtually to renounce his being. And the solemnity wherewith this testimony is entered is very remarkable, verse 7, "There are three that bear record in heaven, the Father, the Word, and the Holy Ghost; and these three are one." The trinity of divine persons, acting distinctly in the unity of the same divine nature, do give this testimony: and they do so by those distinct operations whereby they act in this way and work of God's saving sinners by Jesus Christ; which are at large declared in the gospel. And there is added hereunto a testimony that is immediately applicatory unto the souls of believers, of this sovereign testimony of the holy Trinity; and this is the witness of grace and all sacred ordinances: "There are three that bear witness in earth, the spirit, and the water, and the blood: and these three agree in one," verse 8. They are not at essentially the same in one and the same nature, as are the Father, Word, and Holy Ghost, yet they all absolutely agree in the same testimony; and they do it by that especial efficacy which they have on the souls of believers to assure them of this truth. In this record, so solemnly, so gloriously given and proposed, life and death are set before us. The receiving and embracing of this testimony, with an approbation of the way of salvation testified unto, is that work of faith which secures us of eternal life. On these terms there is reconciliation and agreement made and established between God and men; without which men must perish for ever. So our blessed Saviour affirms, "This is life eternal, that they may know thee" (the Father) "the only true God, and Jesus Christ whom thou hast sent," John xvii. 3. To know the Father as the only true God, to know him as he has sent Jesus Christ to be the only way and means of the salvation of sinners, and to know Jesus Christ as sent by him for that end, is that grace and duty which instates us in a right to eternal life, and initiates us in the possession of it: and this includes that choice and approbation of the way of God for the saving of sinners whereof we speak.

But these things must be more distinctly opened:—

1. The great fundamental difference in religion is concerning the way and means whereby sinners may be saved. From men's different apprehensions hereof arise all other differences about religion; and the first thing that engages men really into any concernment in religion, is an inquiry in their minds how sinners may be saved, or what they shall do themselves to be saved: "What shall we do? what shall we do to be saved?" "What is the way of acceptance with God?" is that inquiry which gives men their first initiation into religion. See Acts ii. 37; xvi. 30; Micah vi. 6-8. This question being once raised in the conscience, an answer must be returned unto it. "I will consider," says the prophet, "what I shall answer when I am reproved," Hab.ii. 1. And there is all the reason in the world that men consider well of a good answer hereunto, without which they must perish for ever; for if they cannot answer themselves here, how do they hope to answer God hereafter? Wherefore, without a sufficient answer always in readiness unto this inquiry, no man can have any hopes of a blessed eternity. Now, the real answer which men return unto themselves is according to the

influence which their minds are under from one or other of the two divine covenants,—that of works or that of grace. And these two covenants, taken absolutely, are inconsistent, and give answers in this case that are directly contradictory to one another: so the apostle declares, Rom.x. 5-9. The one says, "The man that does the works of the law shall live by them; this is the only way whereby you may be saved:" the other wholly waives this return, and puts it all on faith in Christ Jesus. Hence there is great difference and great variety in the answers which men return to themselves on this inquiry; for their consciences will neither hear nor speak any thing but what complies with the covenant whereunto they do belong. These things are reconciled only in the blood of Christ; and how, the apostle declared, Rom.xviii. 3. The greatest part of convinced sinners seem to adhere to the testimony of the covenant of works; and so perish for ever. Nothing will stand us in stead in this matter, nothing will save us, "but the answer of a good conscience towards God, by the resurrection of Jesus Christ," 1 Pet. iii. 21.

2. The way that God has prepared for the saving of sinners is a fruit and product of infinite wisdom, and powerfully efficacious unto its end. As such it is to be received, or it is rejected. It is not enough that we admit of the notions of it as declared, unless we are sensible of divine wisdom and power in it, so as that it may be safely trusted unto. Hereon, upon the proposal of it, falls out

the eternally distinguishing difference among men. Some look upon it and embrace it as the power and wisdom of God; others really reject it as a thing foolish and weak, not meet to be trusted unto. Hereof the apostle gives an account at large, 1 Cor. i. 18-24. And this is mysterious in religion:—the same divine truth is by the same way and means, at the same time, proposed unto sundry persons, all in the same condition, under the same circumstances, all equally concerned in that which is proposed therein: some of them hereon do receive it, embrace it, approve of it, and trust unto it for life and salvation; others despise it, reject it, value it not, trust not unto it. To the one it is the wisdom of God, and the power of God; to the other, weakness and foolishness: as it must of necessity be the one or the other,—it is not capable of a middle state or consideration. It is not a good way unless it be the only way; it is not a safe, it is not the best way, if there be any other; for it is eternally inconsistent with any other. It is the wisdom of God, or it is downright folly. And here, after all our disputes, we must resort unto eternal sovereign grace, making a distinction among them unto whom the gospel is proposed, and the almighty power of actual grace in curing that unbelief which blinds the minds of men, that they can see nothing but folly and weakness in God's way of the saving of sinners. And this unbelief works yet in the most of them unto whom this way of God is proposed in the gospel; they receive it not as an effect of infinite wisdom, and as powerfully efficacious unto its proper end. Some are profligate in the service of their lusts, and regard it not; unto whom may be applied that [saying] of the prophet, "Hear, ye despisers, and wonder, and perish." Some are under the power of darkness and ignorance, so as that they apprehend not, they understand not the mystery of it; for "the light shineth in darkness, and the darkness comprehendeth it not." Some are blinded by Satan, as he is the god of this world, by filling their minds with prejudice, and their hearts with the love of present things, that the light of the glorious gospel of Christ, who is the image of God, cannot shine into them. Some would mix with it their own works, ways, and duties, as they belong unto the first covenant; which are eternally irreconcilable unto this way of God, as the apostle teaches, Rom. x. 3, 4. Hereby does unbelief eternally ruin the souls of men. They do not, they cannot, approve of the way of God for saving sinners proposed in the gospel, as an effect of infinite wisdom and power, which they may safely trust unto, in opposition unto all other ways and means, pretending to be useful unto the same end; and this will give us light into the nature and acting of saving faith, which we inquire after.

3. The whole Scripture, and all divine institutions from the beginning, do testify, in general, that this way of God for the saving of sinners is by commutation, substitution,

atonement, satisfaction, and imputation. This is the language of the first promise, and all the sacrifices of the law founded thereon; this is the language of the Scripture: "There is a way whereby sinners may be saved,—a way that God has found out and appointed." Now, it being the law wherein sinners are concerned, the rule of all things between God and them should seem to be by what they can do or suffer with respect unto that law. "No," says the Scripture, "it cannot be so; for by the deeds of the law no man living shall be justified in the sight of God." Ps. cxliii. 2; Rom. iii. 20; Gal. ii. 16. Neither shall it be by their personal answering of the penalty of the law which they have broken; for they cannot do so, but they must perish eternally: for, "If thou, LORD, shouldest mark iniquities, O Lord, who shall stand?" Ps. cxx. 3. There must therefore be, there is another way, of a different nature and kind from these, for the saving of sinners, or there is no due revelation made of the mind of God in the Scripture. But that there is so, and what it is, is the main design of it to declare: and this is by the substitution of a mediator instead of the sinners that shall be saved, who shall both bear the penalty of the law which they had incurred and fulfill that righteousness which they could not attain unto. This in general is God's way of saving sinners, whether men like it or no: "For what the law could not do, in that it was weak through the flesh, God sending his own Son in the likeness of sinful flesh, and for sin, condemned sin in the flesh; that the righteousness of the law might be fulfilled in us," Rom. viii. 3, 4. See also Heb. v. 5-10. "He made him to be sin for us, who knew no sin; that we might be made the righteousness of God in him," 2 Cor. v. 21. Here unbelief has prevailed with many in this latter age to reject the glory of God herein; but we have vindicated the truth against them sufficiently elsewhere.

4. There are sundry things previously required to give us a clear view of the glory of God in this way of saving sinners: such are, a due consideration of the nature of the fall of our first parents, and of our apostasy from God thereby. I may not stay here to show the nature or aggravations of them; neither can we conceive them aright, much less express them. I only say, that unless we have due apprehensions of the dread and terror of them, of the invasion made on the glory of God, and the confusion brought on the creation by them, we can never discern the reason and glory of rejecting the way of personal righteousness, and the establishing this way of a mediator for the saving of sinners. A due sense of our present infinite distance from God, and the impossibility that there is in ourselves of making any approaches unto him, is of the same consideration; so likewise is that of our utter disability to do any thing that may answer the law, or the holiness and righteousness of God therein,—of our universal unconformity in our natures, hearts, and their acting, unto the nature,

holiness, and will of God. Unless, I say, we have a sense of these things in our minds and upon our consciences, we cannot believe aright, we cannot comprehend the glory of this new way of salvation. And whereas mankind has had a general notion, though no distinct apprehension, of these things, or of some of them, many amongst them have apprehended that there is a necessity of some kind of satisfaction or atonement to be made, that sinners may be freed from the displeasure of God; but when God's way of it was proposed unto them, it was, and is, generally rejected, because "the carnal mind is enmity against God." But when these things are fixed on the soul by sharp and durable convictions, they will enlighten it with due apprehensions of the glory and beauty of God's way of saving sinners.

5. This is the gospel, this is the work of it,— namely, a divine declaration of the way of God for the saving of sinners, through the person, mediation, blood, righteousness, and intercession of Christ. This is that which it reveals, declares, proposes, and tenders unto sinners,— there is a way for their salvation. As this is contained in the first promise, so the truth of every word in the Scripture depends on the supposition of it. Without this, there could be no more intercourse between God and us than is between him and devils. Again, it declares that this way is not by the law or its works,—by the first covenant, or its conditions,—by our own doing or suffering; but it is a new way, found out in and proceeding from

infinite wisdom, love, grace, and goodness,—
namely, by the incarnation of the eternal Son of
God, his susception of the office of a mediator,
doing and suffering in the discharge of it
whatever was needful for the justification and
salvation of sinners, unto his own eternal glory.
See Rom. iii. 24-27; viii. 3, 4; 2 Cor. v. 19-21, etc.
Moreover, the gospel adds, that the only way of
obtaining an interest in this blessed contrivance
of saving sinners by the substitution of Christ, as
the surety of the covenant, and thereon the
imputation of our sins to him, and of his
righteousness unto us, is by faith in him. Here
comes in that trial of faith which we inquire after.
This way of saving sinners being proposed,
offered, and tendered unto us in the gospel, true
and saving faith receives it, approves of it, rests in
it, renounces all other hopes and expectations,
reposing its whole confidence therein. For it is
not proposed unto us merely as a notion of truth,
to be assented to or denied, in which sense all
believe the gospel that are called Christians,—
they do not esteem it a fable; but it is proposed
unto us as that which we ought practically to
close withal, for ourselves to trust alone unto it
for life and salvation. And I shall speak briefly
unto two things:—

I. How does saving faith approve of this way?
on what accounts, and unto what ends?

II. How it does evidence and manifest itself
hereby unto the comfort of believers.

I.

How does saving faith approve of this way? on what accounts, and unto what ends?

FIRST, It approves of it, as that which every way becomes God to find out, to grant, and propose: so speaks the apostle, Heb.ii. 10, "It became him, in bringing many sons unto glory, to make the Captain of their salvation perfect through sufferings." That becomes God, is worthy of him, is to be owned concerning him, which answers unto his infinite wisdom, goodness, grace, holiness, and righteousness, and nothing else. This faith discerns, judges, and determines concerning this way,—namely, that it is every way worthy of God, and answers all the holy properties of his nature. This is called "The light of the knowledge of the glory of God in the face of Jesus Christ," 2 Cor. iv. 6.

This discovery of the glory of God in this way is made unto faith alone, and by it alone it is embraced. The not discerning of it, and thereon the want of an acquiescence in it, is that unbelief which ruins the souls of men. The reason why men do not embrace the way of salvation tendered in the gospel, is because they do not see nor understand how full it is of divine glory, how it becomes God, is worthy of him, and answers all the perfections of his nature. Their minds are blinded, that the light of the glorious gospel of

Christ, who is the image of God, does not shine unto them, 2 Cor. iv. 4. And so they deal with this way of God as if it were weakness and folly.

Herein consists the essence and life of faith:—It sees, discerns, and determines, that the way of salvation of sinners by Jesus Christ proposed in the gospel, is such as becomes God and all his divine excellencies to find out, appoint, and propose unto us. And herein does it properly give glory to God, which is its peculiar work and excellency, Rom. iv. 20; herein it rests and refreshes itself. In particular, faith herein rejoices in the manifestation of the infinite wisdom of God. A view of the wisdom of God acting itself by his power in the works of creation (for in wisdom he made them all), is the sole reason of ascribing glory unto him in all natural worship, whereby we glorify him as God; and a due apprehension of the infinite wisdom of God in the new creation, in the way of saving sinners by Jesus Christ, is the foundation of all spiritual, evangelical ascription of glory to God. It was the design of God, in a peculiar way, to manifest and glorify his wisdom in this work. Christ crucified is the "power of God, and the wisdom of God," 1 Cor. i. 24; and "all the treasures of wisdom and knowledge are hid in him," Col. ii. 3. All the treasures of divine wisdom are laid up in Christ, and laid out about him, as to be manifested unto faith in and by the gospels He designed herein to make known his "manifold wisdom," Eph. iii. 9,10.

Wherefore, according to our apprehension and admiration of the wisdom of God in the constitution of this way of salvation is our faith, and no otherwise; where that does not appear unto us, where our minds are not affected with it, there is no faith at all. I cannot stay here to reckon up the especial instances of divine wisdom herein. Somewhat I have attempted towards it in other writings; and I shall only say at present, that the foundation of this whole work and way, in the incarnation of the eternal Son of God, is so glorious an effect of infinite wisdom, as the whole blessed creation will admire to eternity. This of itself bespeaks this way and work divine. Herein the glory of God shines in the face of Jesus Christ. This is of God alone; this is that which becomes him; that which nothing but infinite wisdom could extend unto. Whilst faith lives in a due apprehension of the wisdom of God in this, and the whole superstruction of this way, on this foundation it is safe.

Goodness, love, grace, and mercy, are other properties of the divine nature, wherein it is gloriously amiable. "God is love;" there is none God but he. Grace and mercy are among the principal titles which he everywhere assumes to himself; and it was his design to manifest them all to the utmost in this work and way of saving sinners by Christ, as is everywhere declared in the Scripture. And all these lie open to the eye of faith herein: it sees infinite goodness, love, and grace, in this way, such as becomes God, such as can reside in none but him; which it therefore rests and rejoices in, 1 Pet. i. 8. In adherence unto, and approbation of, this way of salvation, as expressive of these perfections of the divine nature, does faith act itself continually. Where unbelief prevails, the mind has no view of the glory that is in this way of salvation, in that it is so becoming of God and all his holy properties, as the apostle declares, 2 Cor. iv. 4. And where it is so, whatever is pretended, men cannot cordially receive it and embrace it; for they know not the reason for which it ought to be so embraced: they see no form nor comeliness in Christ, who is the life and centre of this way, "no beauty for which he should be desired," Isa. liii. 2. Hence, in the first preaching of it, it was "unto the Jews a stumbling-block, and unto the Greeks foolishness;" for by reason of their unbelief they could not see it to be, what it is, "the power of God, and the wisdom of God;" and so it must be esteemed, or be accounted folly. Yea, from the same unbelief it is that at this day the very notion of the truth herein is rejected by many, even all those who are called Socinians, and all that adhere unto them in the disbelief of supernatural mysteries. They cannot see a suitableness in this way of salvation unto the glory of God,—as no unbeliever can; and therefore those of them who do not oppose directly the doctrine of it, yet do make no use of it unto its proper end. Very few of them, comparatively, who profess the truth of the gospel, have an experience of the power of it unto their own salvation.

But here true faith stands invincibly,—hereby it will evidence its truth and sincerity in the midst of all temptations, and the most dismal conflicts it has with them; yea, against the perplexing power and charge of sin thence arising. From this stronghold it will not be driven; whilst the soul can exercise faith herein,—namely, in steadily choosing, embracing, and approving of God's way of saving sinners by Jesus Christ, as that wherein he will be eternally glorified, because it is suited unto, and answers all the perfections of, his nature, is that which every way becomes him,—it will have wherewith to relieve itself in all its trials. For this is faith, this is saving faith, which will not fail us. That faith which works in the soul a gracious persuasion of the excellency of this way, by a sight of the glory of the wisdom, power, grace, love, and goodness of God in it, so as to be satisfied with it, as the best, the only way of coming unto God, with a renunciation of all other ways and means unto that end, will at all times evidence its nature and sincerity. And this is that which gives the soul rest and satisfaction, as unto its entrance into glory, upon its departure out of this world. It is a great thing, to apprehend in a due manner that a poor soul that has been guilty of many sins, leaving the body, it may be, under great pain, distress, and anguish, it may be by outward violence, should be immediately admitted and received into the glorious presence of God, with all the holy attendants of his throne, there to enjoy rest and blessedness for evermore.

But here also faith discerns and approves of this great, of this ineffable, divine operation, as that which becomes the infinite greatness of that wisdom and grace which first designed it, the glorious efficacy of the mediation of Christ, and the excellency of the sanctification of the Holy Spirit, without any expectation from any thing in itself, as a cause meritorious of an admission into this glory. Neither did ever any man know what it is, or desire it in a due manner, who looked for any desert of it in himself, or conceived any proportion between it and what he is or has done in this world. Hence some of those who have not this faith have invented another state, after men are gone out of this world, to make them meet for heaven, which they call purgatory; for on what grounds a man should expect an entrance into glory, on his departure out of this world, they understand not. Let them who are exercised with temptations and dejections bring their faith unto this trial; and this is the case, in various degrees, of us all:—First, then, examine strictly by the word whether this be a true description of the nature and acting of saving faith. Sundry things are supposed or asserted in it, as—

1. That the way of saving sinners by Jesus Christ is the principal effect of divine wisdom, power, goodness, love, and grace.

2. That the design of the gospel is to manifest, declare, and testify that so it is, and so to make known the glory of God therein.

3. That saving faith is that act, duty, and work of the soul, whereby we receive the record of God concerning these things, [and] do ascribe the glory of them all unto him, as discovering it in the way of life proposed unto us.

4. That hereon it proceeds unto a renunciation of all other ways, means, hopes, reliefs, in opposition unto this way, or in conjunction with it, as unto acceptance with God in life and salvation. I say, in the first place, examine these things strictly by the word; and if they appear to be (as they are) sacred, evangelical, fundamental truths, be not moved from them, be not shaken in them, by any temptation whatever.

And, in the next place, bring your faith to the trial on these principles: What do you judge concerning God's way of saving sinners by Jesus Christ, as proposed in the gospel? Are you satisfied in it, that it is such as becomes God, and answers all the glorious attributes of his nature? Would you have any other way proposed in the room of it? Can you, will you, commit the eternal welfare of your souls unto the grace and faithfulness of God in this way, so as that you have no desire to be saved any other way? Does the glory of God in any measure shine forth unto you in the face of Jesus Christ? Do you find a secret joy in your hearts upon the satisfaction you take in the proposal of this way unto you by the gospel? Do you, in all your fears and temptations, in all approaches of death, renounce all other reserves and reliefs, and retake your whole confidence unto this way alone, and the representation of God made therein? Herein lies that faith, and its exercise, which will be an anchor unto your souls in all their trials.

And this is the first and principal ground, or reason, whereon faith, divine and saving, does accept, embrace, and approve of the way of God's saving sinners by Jesus Christ,—namely, because it is such as does become him, and every way answer unto all the holy properties of his nature, which are manifested and glorified therein. And where faith does approve of it on this ground and reason, it does evidence itself to be truly evangelical, unto the supportment and comfort of them in whom it is.

Secondly, It does so approve of this way as that which it finds suited unto the whole design and all the desires of an enlightened soul. So when our Lord Jesus Christ compares the kingdom of God (which is this way of salvation) unto a treasure and a precious pearl, he affirms that those who found them had great joy and the highest satisfaction, as having attained that which suited their desires, and gave rest unto their minds. A soul enlightened with the knowledge of the truth, and made sensible of its own condition by spiritual conviction, has two predominant desires and aims, whereby it is wholly regulated,—the one is, that God may be gloried; and the other, that itself may be eternally saved. Nor can it forego either of these desires, nor are they separable in any enlightened soul. It can never cease in either of these desires, and that to the highest degree. The whole world cannot dispossess an enlightened mind of either of them. Profligate sinners have no concernment in the former; no, nor yet those who are under legal convictions, if they have wherewithal received no spiritual light. They would be saved; but for the glory of God therein, he may look to that himself,—they are not concerned in it: for that which they mean by salvation is nothing but a freedom from external misery. This they would have, whether God be [glorified] or no; of what is salvation truly they have no desire.

But the first beam of spiritual light and grace instates an indefatigable desire of the glory of God in the minds and souls of them in whom it is. Without this the soul knows not how to desire its own salvation. I may say, it would not be saved in a way wherein God should not be glorified; for without that, whatever its state should be, it would not be that which we call salvation. The exaltation of the glory of God belongs essentially thereunto; it consists in the beholding and enjoyment of that glory. This desire, therefore, is immovably fixed in the mind and soul of every enlightened person; he can admit of no proposal of eternal things that is inconsistent with it. But, moreover, in every such person there is a ruling desire of his own salvation. It is natural unto him, as a creature made for eternity; it is inseparable from him, as he is a convinced sinner. And the clearer the light of any one is in the nature of this salvation, the more is this desire heightened and confirmed in him.

Here, then, lies the inquiry,—namely, how these two prevalent desires may be reconciled and satisfied in the same mind? For, as we are sinners, there seems to be an inconsistency between them. The glory of God, in his justice and holiness, requires that sinners should die and perish eternally. So speaks the law; this is the language of conscience, and the voice of all our fears: wherefore for a sinner to desire, in the first place, that God may be glorified is to desire that himself may be damned. Which of these desires shall the sinner cleave unto? Unto whether of them shall he give the preeminence? Shall he cast off all hopesand desires of his own salvation, and be content to perish forever? This he cannot do; God does not require it of him,—he has given him the contrary in charge whilst he is in this world. Shall he, then, desire that God may part with and lose his glory, so as that, one way or other, he may be saved? Bring himself unto an unconcernment what becomes of it? This can be no more in an enlightened mind than it can cease to desire its own salvation. But how to reconcile these things in himself a sinner finds not.

Here, therefore, the glory of this way represents itself unto the faith of every believer. It not only brings these desires into a perfect consistency and harmony, but makes them to increase and promote one another. The desire of God's glory increases the desire of our own salvation; and the desire of our own salvation enlarges and inflames the desire of glorifying God therein and thereby. These things are brought into a perfect consistency and mutual subserviency in the blood of Christ, Rom.iii. 24-26; for this way is that which God has found out, in infinite wisdom, to glorify himself in the salvation of sinners. There is not any thing wherein the glory of God does or may consist, but in this way is reconciled unto, and consistent with, the salvation of the chiefest of sinners. There is no property of his nature but is gloriously exalted in and by it. An answer is given in it unto all the objections of the law against the consistency of the glory of God and the salvation of sinners. It pleads his truth in his threatening, in the sanction of the law, with the curse annexed;—it pleads his righteousness, holiness, and severity, all engaged to destroy sinners;—it pleads the instance of God's dealing with the angels that sinned, and calls in the witness of conscience to testify the truth of all its allegations: but there is a full and satisfactory answer given unto this whole plea of the law in this way of salvation. God declares in it, and by it, how he has provided for the satisfaction of all these things, and the exaltation of his glory in them; as we shall see immediately. Here true faith will fix itself in all its distresses. "Whatever," says the soul, "be my state and condition, whatever be my fears and perplexities, whatever oppositions I meet withal, yet I see in Jesus Christ, in the glass of the gospel, that there is no inconsistency between the glory of God and my salvation. That otherwise insuperable difficulty laid by the law in the way of my life and comfort, is utterly removed." Whilst faith keeps this hold in the soul, with a constant approbation of this way of salvation by Christ, as that which gives [such] a consistency unto both its governing desires, that it shall not need forego either of them,—so as to be contented to be damned that God may be glorified, as some have spoken, or to desire salvation without a due regard unto the glory of God,—it will be an anchor to stay the soul in all its storms and distresses. Some benefit which will certainly ensue hereon we may briefly mention.

1. The soul will be hereby preserved from ruining despair, in all the distresses that may befall it. Despair is nothing but a prevalent apprehension of [the] mind that the glory of God and a man's salvation are inconsistent;—that God cannot be just, true, holy, or righteous, if he in whom that apprehension is may be saved. Such a person does conclude that his salvation is impossible,because, one way or other, it is inconsistent with the glory of God; for nothing else can render it impossible. Hence arises in the mind an utter dislike of God, with revengeful thoughts against him for being what he is. This cuts off all endeavours of reconciliation, yea, begets an abhorrence of all the means of it, as

those which are weak, foolish, and insufficient. Such are Christ and his cross unto men under such apprehensions; they judge them unable to reconcile the glory of God and their salvation. Then is a soul in an open entrance into hell. From this cursed frame and ruin the soul is safely preserved by faith's maintaining in the mind and heart a due persuasion of the consistency and harmony that is between the glory of God and its own salvation. Whilst this persuasion is prevalent in it, although it cannot attain any comfortable assurance of an especial interest in it, yet it cannot but love, honour, value, and cleave unto this way, adoring the wisdom and grace of God in it; which is an act and evidence of saving faith. See Ps. cxxx. 3,4. Yea,—

2. It will preserve the soul from heartless despondencies. Many in their temptations, darknesses, fears, surprisals by sin, although they fall [not] into ruining desperation, yet they fall under such desponding fears and various discouragements, as keep them off from a vigorous endeavour after a recovery: and hereon, for want of the due exercise of grace, they grow weaker and darker every day, and are in danger to pine away in their sins. But where faith keeps the soul constant unto the approbation of God's way of saving sinners, as that wherein the glory of God and its own salvation are not only fully reconciled but made inseparable, it will stir up all graces unto a due exercise, and the diligent performance of all duties, whereby it may obtain a refreshing sense of a personal interest in it.

3. It will keep the heart full of kindness towards God; whence love and gracious hope will spring. It is impossible but that a soul overwhelmed with a sense of sin, and thereon filled with self-condemnation, but if it has a view of the consistency of the glory of God with its deliverance and salvation, through a free contrivance of infinite wisdom and grace, it must have such kindness for him, such gracious thoughts of him, as will beget and kindle in it both love and hope, as Mic. vii. 18-20; Ps. lxxv. 8; 1 Tim. i. 15.

4. A steady continuance in the approbation of God's way of salvation, on the reason mentioned, will lead the mind into that exercise of faith which both declares its nature and is the spring of all the saving benefits which we receive by it. Now, this is such a spiritual light into, and discovery of, the revelation and declaration made in the gospel of the wisdom, love, grace, and mercy of God in Christ Jesus, and the way of the communication of the effect of them unto sinners by him, as that the soul finds them suited unto and able for the pardon of its own sins, its righteousness and salvation; so as that it places its whole trust and confidence for these ends therein.

This being the very life of faith, that act and exercise of it whereby we are justified and saved, and whereby it evidences its truth and sincerity against all temptations, I shall insist a little on the explanation of the description of it now given.

And there are three things in it, or required unto it:—

(1.) A spiritual light into, and discovery of, the revelation and declaration made in the gospel of the wisdom, love, grace, and mercy of God in Christ Jesus. It is not a mere assent unto the truth of the revelation or authority of the revealer;— this, indeed, is supposed and included in it; but it adds thereunto a spiritual discerning, perception, and understanding of the things themselves revealed and declared; without which, a bare assent unto the truth of the revelation is of no advantage. This is called "The light of the knowledge of the glory of God in the face of Jesus Christ," 2 Cor. iv. 6; the increase whereof in all believers the apostle does earnestly pray for, Eph. i. 15-20. So we discern spiritual things in a spiritual manner; and hence arises "the full assurance of understanding, to the acknowledgment of the mystery of God, and of the Father, and of Christ," Col. ii. 2; or a spiritual sense of the power, glory, and beauty of the things contained in this mystery: so to know Christ as to know "the power of his resurrection, and the fellowship of his sufferings," Phil. iii. 10. Faith affects the mind with an ineffable sense, taste, experience, and acknowledgment of the greatness, the glory, the power, the beauty of the things revealed and proposed in this way of salvation. The soul in it is enabled to see and understand that all the things belonging unto it are such as become God, his wisdom, goodness, and love; as was before declared. And a spiritual light enabling hereunto is of the essence of saving faith; unless this be in us, we do not, we cannot, give glory to God in any assent unto the truth. And faith is that grace which God has prepared, fitted, and suited, to give unto him the glory that is his due in the work of our redemption and salvation.

(2.) Upon this spiritual light into this revelation of God and his glory, in this way of saving sinners, the mind by faith finds and sees that all things in it are suited unto its own justification and salvation in particular, and that the power of God is in them to make them effectual unto that end. This is that act and work of faith whereon the whole blessed event does depend. It will not avail a man to see all sorts of viands and provisions, if they be no way suited unto his appetite, nor meet for his nourishment; nor will it be unto a man's spiritual advantage to take a view of the excellencies of the gospel, unless he find them suited unto his condition. And this is the hardest task and work that faith has to go through with.

Faith is not an especial assurance of a man's own justification and salvation by Christ; that it will produce, but not until another step or two in its progress be over: but faith is a satisfactory persuasion that the way of God proposed in the gospel is fitted, suited, and able to save the soul in particular that does believe,—not only that it is a blessed way to save sinners in general, but that it is such a way to save him in particular. So is this matter stated by the apostle, 1 Tim. i. 15, "This is a faithful saying, and worthy of all acceptation," or approbation, "that Christ Jesus came into the world to save sinners, of whom I am chief." His faith does not abide here, nor confine itself unto this, that Christ Jesus came into the world to save sinners, that this is the holy and blessed way of God for the salvation of sinners in general; but he puts in for his own particular interest in that way: "It is God's way, fitted, and suited, and able to save me, who am the chiefest of sinners." And this, as was said, is the greatest and the most difficult work of faith; for we suppose, concerning the person who is to believe,—

[1.] That he is really and effectually convinced of the sin of [our] nature, of our apostasy from God therein, the loss of his image, and the direful effects that ensue thereon.

[2.] That he has due apprehensions of the holiness and severity of God, of the sanction and curse of the law, with a right understanding of the nature of sin and its demerit.

[3.] That he have a full conviction of his own actual sins, with all their aggravations, from their greatness, their number, and all sorts of circumstances.

[4.] That he has a sense of the guilt of secret or unknown sins, which have been multiplied by that continual proneness unto sin which he finds working in him.

[5.] That he seriously consider what it is to appear before the judgment-seat of God, to receive a sentence for eternity, with all other things of the like nature, inseparable from him as a sinner.

When it is really thus with any man, he shall find it the hardest thing in the world, and clogged with the most difficulties, for him to believe that the way of salvation proposed unto him is suited, fitted, and every way able to save him in particular,—to apprehend it such as none of his objections can rise up against, or stand before. But this is that, in the second place, that the faith of God's elect will do: it will enable the soul to discern and satisfy itself that there is in this way of God every thing that is needful unto its own salvation. And this it will do on a spiritual understanding and due consideration of,—

[1.] The infiniteness of that wisdom, love, grace, and mercy, which is the original or sovereign cause of the whole way, with the ample declaration and confirmation made of them in the gospel.

[2.] Of the unspeakably glorious way and means for the procuring and communicating unto us of all the effects of that wisdom, grace, and mercy,—namely, the incarnation and mediation of the Son of God, in his oblation and intercession.

[3.] Of the great multitude and variety of precious promises, engaging the truth, faithfulness, and power of God, for the communication of righteousness and salvation from those springs, by that means. I say, on the just consideration of these things, with all other encouragements wherewith they are accompanied, the soul concludes by faith that there is salvation for itself in particular, to be attained in that way.

(3.) The last act of faith, in the order of nature, is the soul's acquiescence in, and trust unto, this way of salvation for itself and its own eternal condition, with a renunciation of all other ways and means for that end. And because Jesus Christ, in his person, mediation, and righteousness, is the life and centre of this way, as he in whom alone God will glorify his wisdom, love, grace, and mercy,—as he who has purchased, procured, and wrought all this salvation for us,—whose righteousness is imputed unto us for our justification, and who in the discharge of his office does actually bestow it upon us,—he is the proper and immediate object of faith, in this act of trust and affiance. This is that which is called in the Scripture believing in Christ,— namely, the trusting unto him alone for life and salvation, as the whole of divine wisdom and grace is administered by him unto these ends. For this we come unto him, we receive him, we believe in him, we trust him, we abide in him; with all those other ways whereby our faith in him is expressed. And this is the second ground or reason whereon faith does close with, embrace, and approve of God's way of saving sinners; whereby it will evidence itself, unto the comfort of them in whom it is, in the midst of all their trials and temptations.

Thirdly, Faith approves of this way, as that which makes the glory of God, in the giving and the sanction of the law, to be as eminently conspicuous as if it had been perfectly fulfilled by every one of us in our own persons. The law was a just representation of the righteousness and holiness of God; and the end for which it was given was, that it might be the means and instrument of the eternal exaltation of his glory in these holy properties of his nature. Let no man imagine that God has laid aside this law, as a thing of no more use; or that he will bear a diminution of that glory, or any part of it, which he designed in the giving of it. Heaven and earth shall pass away, but no jot or little of the law shall do so. No believer can desire, or be pleased with, his own salvation, unless the glory of God designed by the law be secured. He cannot desire that God should forego any part of his glory that he might be saved. Yea, this is that on the account whereof he principally rejoices in his own salvation,—namely, that it is that wherein God will be absolutely, universally, and eternally glorified. Now, in this way of saving sinners by Jesus Christ, by mercy, pardon, and the righteousness of another (of all which the law knows nothing), faith does see and understand how all that glory which God designed in the giving of the law is eternally secured and preserved entire, without eclipse or diminution. The way whereby this is done is declared in the gospel. See Rom. iii. 24-26; viii. 2-4; x. 3, 4. Hereby faith is enabled to answer all the challenges and charges of the law, with all its pleas for the vindication of divine justice, truth and holiness; it has that to offer which gives it the utmost satisfaction in all its pleas for God: so is this answer managed, Rom.viii. 32-34.

And this is the first way whereby the faith of God's elect does evidence itself in the minds and consciences of them that do believe, in the midst of all their contests with sin, their trials and temptations, to their relief and comfort,— namely, the closing with, and approbation of, God's way of saving sinners by Jesus Christ, on the grounds and reasons which have been declared.

II

The second evidence of the faith of God's elect

THE second way whereby true faith does evidence itself in the souls and consciences of believers, unto their supportment and comfort under all their conflicts with sin, in all their trials and temptations, is by a constant approbation of the revelation of the will of God in the Scripture concerning our holiness, and the obedience unto himself which he requires of us. This faith will never forego, whatever trials it may undergo, whatever darkness the mind may fall into; this it will abide by in all extremities. And that it may appear to be a peculiar effect or work of saving faith, some things are to be premised and considered:—

1. There is in all men by nature a light enabling them to judge of the difference that is between what is morally good and what is evil, especially in things of more than ordinary importance. This light is not attained or acquired by us; we are not taught it, we do not learn it: it is born with us, and inseparable from us; it prevents [exists previously to] consideration and reflection, working naturally, and in a sort necessarily, in the first acting of our souls. And the discerning power of this light, as to the moral nature of

men's actions, is accompanied inseparably with a judgment that they make concerning themselves as unto what they do of the one kind or other, and that with respect unto the superior judgment of God about the same things. This the apostle expressly ascribes unto the Gentiles, who had not the law, Rom. ii. 14, 15: "The Gentiles, which have not the law, do by nature the things contained in the law, these, having not the law, are a law unto themselves: which show the work of the law written in their hearts, their consciences also bearing witness, and their thoughts the meanwhile accusing or else excusing one another." This is a most exact description of a natural conscience, in both the powers of it; it discerns that good and evil which is commanded and forbidden in the law, and it passes an acquitting or condemning judgment and sentence, according to what men have done.

Wherefore, this approbation of duties in things moral is common unto all men. The light whereby it is guided may be variously improved, as it was in some of the Gentiles; and it may be stifled in some, until it seem to be quite extinguished, until they become like the beasts that perish. And where the discerning power of this light remains, yet, through a continual practice of sin and obduracy therein, the judging power of it as unto all its efficacy may be lost: so the apostle declares concerning them who are judicially hardened and given up unto sin, Rom. i. 32, "These, knowing the judgment of God, that they which commit such things are worthy of death, not only do the same, but have pleasure in them that do them." They still discern what is evil and sinful, and know what is the judgment of God conceding such things; but yet the love of sin and custom in sinning do so far prevail in them, as to contemn both their own light and God's judgment, so as to delight in what is contrary unto them. These the apostle describes, Eph. iv. 19, "Being past feeling" (all sense of convictions), "they have given themselves over unto lasciviousness, to work all uncleanness with greediness;" such as the world is filled withal at this day. This is not that approbation of obedience which we inquire after; it is, in some measure, in the worst of men, nor has it any likeness unto that duty of faith which we treat of, as will immediately appear.

2. There is a further knowledge of good and evil by the law, and this is also accompanied with a judgment acquitting or condemning; for the law has the same judging power and authority over men that their own consciences have,—namely, the authority of God himself. The law is to sinners as the tree of knowledge of good and evil,—it opens their eyes to see the nature of what they have done; for "by the law is the knowledge of sin," Rom.iii. 20: and so is the knowledge of duty also; for it is the adequate rule of all duty. There is, I say, a knowledge and conviction of duty and sin communicated unto men by the law, and those far more clear and

distinct than what is or can be found in men from the mere light of nature; for it extends to more instances, that being generally lost where it is alone, as unto many important duties and sins; and it declares the nature of every sin and duty far more clearly than natural light of itself can do.

And this knowledge of good and evil by the law may be so improved in the minds of men as to press them unto a performance of all known duties, and an abstinence from all known sins, with a judgment on them all. But yet herein does not consist that approbation of holiness and obedience which faith will produce; for,—

(1.) As unto approbation or condemnation of good or evil: that which is by the law is particular, or has respect unto particular duties and sins, according as occasion does present them; and extends not unto the whole law absolutely, and all that is required in it. I do not say it is always partial; there is a legal sincerity that may have respect unto all known duties and sins, though it be very rare. Hardly shall we find a person merely under the power of the law, who does not evidence an indulgence unto some sin, and a neglect of some duties: but such a thing there may be; it was in Paul, in his pharisaism,—he was, "touching the righteousness which is in the law, blameless," Phil. iii. 6. He allowed not himself in any known sin, nor in the neglect of any known duty; nor could others charge him with any defect therein,—he was blameless. But where this is, still this approbation or condemnation is particular,—that is, they do respect particular duties and sins as they do occur; there is not a respect in them unto the whole righteousness and holiness of the law, as we shall see. Wherefore, a man may approve of every duty in its season as it is offered unto him, or when at any time he thinks of it by an act of his fixed judgment; and so, on the contrary, as unto sin; and yet come short of that approbation of holiness and righteousness which we inquire after.

(2.) It is not accompanied with a love of the things themselves that are good, as they are so, and a hatred of the contrary; for the persons in whom it is do not, cannot, "delight in the law of God after the inward man," as Rom. vii. 22, so as to approve of it, and all that is contained in it, cleaving to them with love and delight. They may have a love for this or that duty, and a hatred of the contrary, but it is on various considerations, suited unto their convictions and circumstances; but it is not on the account of its formal nature, as good or evil. Wherefore,—

(3.) No man, without the light of saving faith, can constantly and universally approve of the revelation of the will of God, as unto our holiness and obedience.

To make this evident, which is the foundation of our present discovery of the acting of saving faith, we must consider,—[1.] What it is that is to be approved. [2.] What this approbation is, or wherein it does consist:—

[1.] That which is to be approved is the holiness and obedience which God requires in us, our natures, and actions, and accepts from us, or accepts in ups. It is not particular duties as they occur unto us, taken alone and by themselves, but the universal correspondence of our natures and actions unto the will of God. The Scripture gives us various descriptions of it, because of the variety of graces and gracious operations which concur therein. We may here mention some of its principal concerns, having handled the nature of it at large elsewhere; for it may he considered,— 1st. As unto its foundation, spring, and causes: and this is the universal renovation of our natures into the image of God, Eph. iv. 24; or the change of our whole souls, in all their faculties and powers, into his likeness, whereby we become new creatures, or the workmanship of God created in Christ Jesus unto good works, 2 Cor. v. 17, Eph.ii. 10; wherein we are originally and formally sanctified throughout, in our "whole spirit, and soul, and body," 1 Thess. v. 23. It is the whole law of God written in our hearts, transforming them into the image of the divine holiness, represented therein. And this, next unto the blood of Christ and his righteousness, is the principal spring of peace, rest, and complacency, in and unto the souls of believers: it is their joy and satisfaction to find themselves restored unto a likeness and conformity unto God, as we shall see further immediately. And where there is not some gracious sense and experience hereof, there is nothing but disorder and confusion in the soul; nothing can give it a sweet composure, a satisfaction in itself, a complacency with what it is, but a spiritual sense of this renovation of the image of God in it.

2dly. It may be considered as unto its permanent principle in the mind and affections; and this, because of its near relation unto Christ, its conjunction with him, and derivation from him, is sometimes said to be Christ himself. Hence we live, yet not so much we as Christ lives in us, Gal. ii. 20; for "without him we can do nothing," John xv. 5; for "he is our life," Col. iii. 4. As it resides in believers, it is a permanent principle of spiritual life, light, love, and power, acting in the whole soul and all the faculties of the mind, enabling them to cleave unto God with purpose of heart, and to live unto him in all the acts and duties of spiritual life: this is that whereby the Holy Ghost is "in them a well of water, springing up into everlasting life," John iv. 14. It is the spirit that is born of the Spirit; it is the divine nature, whereof we are made partakers by the promises; it is a principle of victorious faith and love, with all graces any way requisite unto duties of holy obedience; as to the matter or manner of their performance, enabling the soul unto all the acts of the life of God, with delight, joy, and complacency. This it is in its nature. However, as unto degrees of its operation and manifestation, it may be very low and weak in some true believers, at least for a season; but there are none who are really so, but there is in them a spiritually vital principle of obedience, or of living unto God, that is participant of the nature of that which we have described; and if it be attended unto, it will evidence itself in its power and operations unto the gracious refreshment and satisfaction of the soul wherein it is. And there are few who are so destitute of those evidences but that they are able to say, "Whereas I was blind, now I see, though I know not how my eyes were opened; whereas I was dead, I find motions of a new life in me, in breathing after grace, in hungering and thirsting after righteousness, though I know not how I was quickened."

3dly. It may be considered as unto its disposition, inclinations, and motions. These are the first acting of a vital principle; as the first acting of sin are called "the motions of sin" working in our members, Rom.vii. 5. Such motions and inclinations unto obedience do work in the minds of believers, from this principle of holiness; it produces in them a constant, invariable disposition unto all duties of the life of God. It is a new nature, and a nature cannot be without suitable inclinations and motions; and this new spiritual disposition consists in a constant complacency of mind in that which is good and according to the will of God, in an adherence by love unto it, in a readiness and fixedness of mind with respect unto particular duties. In brief, it is that which David describes in the 119th Psalm throughout, and that which is figuratively foretold concerning the efficacy of the grace of the gospel in changing the natures and dispositions of those that are partakers of it, Isa. xi. 6-8.

This every believer may ordinarily find in himself; for although this disposition may be variously weakened, opposed, interrupted by indwelling sin, and the power of temptation; though it may be impaired by a neglect of the stirring up and exercise of the principle of spiritual life, in all requisite graces, on all occasions; yet it will still be working in them, and will fill the mind with a constant discipline with itself, when it is not observed, followed, improved. No believer shall ever have peace in his own mind, who has not some experience of a universal disposition unto all holiness and godliness in his mind and soul: herein consists that love of the law, of which it is said those in whom it is have "great peace, and nothing shall offend them," Ps. i. 19, 165; it is that wherein their souls find much complacency.

4thly. It may be considered with respect unto all the acts, duties, and works, internal and external, wherein our actual obedience does consist. Being, on the principles mentioned, made free from sin, and becoming the servants of God, believers herein have their "fruit unto holiness," whereof "the end is everlasting life," Rom. vi. 22. This I need not stay to describe. Sincerity in every duty, and universality with respect unto all duties, are the properties of it.

"This is the will of God, even your sanctification," 1 Thess. iv. 3; that "holiness, without which no man shall see the Lord," Heb. xii. 14; "that good, and acceptable, and perfect will of Cod" which we are to approve, Rom. xii. 2.

[2.] Our next inquiry is, what is that approbation of this way of holiness which we place as an evidence of saving faith? And I say, it is such as arises from experience, and is accompanied with choice, delight, and acquiescence; it is the acting of the soul in a delightful adherence unto the whole will of God; it is a resolved judgment of the beauty and excellency of that holiness and obedience which the gospel reveals and requires, and that on the grounds which shall be immediately declared, and the nature thereof therein more fully opened. This approbation cannot be in any unregenerate person, who is not under the conduct of saving faith, who is destitute of the light of it. So the apostle assures us, Rom. vii. 7, "The carnal mind is enmity against God: for it is not subject to the law of God, neither indeed can be." Whatever work it may have wrought in it, or upon it, yet, whilst it is carnal or unrenewed, it has a radical enmity unto the law of God; which is the frame of heart which stands in direct opposition unto this approbation. It may think well of this or that duty, from its convictions and other considerations, and so attend unto their performance; but the law itself, in the universal holiness which it requires, it does utterly dislike: those in whom it is are "alienated from the life of God through the ignorance that is in them," Eph. iv. 18. This life of God is that holiness and obedience which he requires of us in their principles and duties; and to be alienated from it is to dislike and disapprove of it: and such is the frame of mind in all unregenerate persons.

Having thus prepared the way, I return unto the declaration and confirmation of the assertion, namely,—

That true and saving faith, in all storms and temptations, in all darknesses and distresses, will evidence itself unto the comfort and supportment of them in whom it is, by a constant, universal approbation of the whole will of God, concerning our holiness and obedience, both in general and in every particular instance of it.

We may a little explain it:—

1. Faith will not suffer the mind, on any occasion or temptation, to entertain the least dislike of this way of holiness, or of any thing that belongs unto it. The mind may sometimes,

through temptations, fall under apprehensions that one shall be eternally ruined for want of a due compliance with it; this makes it displeased with itself, but not with the obedience required. Rom.vii. 10,12, "The commandment, which was ordained to life, I found to be unto death; but the law is holy, and the commandment holy, and just, and good." "However it be with me, whatever becomes of me, though I die and perish, yet the law is holy, just, and good." It dislikes nothing in the will of God, though it cannot attain unto a compliance with it. Sometimes the conscience is under perplexities and rebukes for sin; sometimes the mind is burdened by the tergiversation of the flesh unto duties that are cross unto its inclinations and interests; sometimes the world threatens the utmost dangers unto the performance of some duties of religion: but none of these are able to provoke the soul that is under the conduct of faith to dislike, to think hard of, any of those ways and duties whence these difficulties arise. And,—

2. As it will not dislike any thing in this way of holiness, so it will not desire on any occasion that there should be any alteration in it, or any abatement of it, or of any thing required in it. Naaman the Syrian liked well of the worship of the true God in general; but he would have an abatement of duty as to one instance, in compliance with his earthly interest, which discovered his hypocrisy. Such imaginations may befall the minds of men, that if they might be

excused, in this or that instance, unto duties that are dangerous and troublesome (like profession in the times of persecution), or might be indulged in this or that sin, which either their inclinations are very prone unto, or their secular interest do call for, they should do well enough with all other things. Accordingly, the practice of many does answer their inclination and desire. They will profess religion and obedience unto God, but will keep back part of the price;—will hide a wedge in their tents, through indulgence unto some corruption, or dislike of some duties in their circumstances: they would give unto themselves the measure of their obedience. And according as men's practice is, so do they desire that things indeed should be, that that practice should please God which pleased them. This faith abhors; the soul that is under the conduct of it is not capable of any one desire that any thing were otherwise than it is in the will of God concerning our holiness and obedience, no more than it can desire that God should not be what he is. No; though any imagination should arise in it, that by some change and abatement in some instances it might be saved, which now is uncertain whether that be so or no, it will admit of no such composition, but will choose to stand or fall unto the entire will of God. We shall therefore, in the next place, proceed to inquire on what grounds it is that faith does thus approve of the whole will of God, as unto our holiness and obedience; as also, how it evidences itself so to do. And these grounds are two:—the one respecting God; the other, our own souls. First, Faith looks on the holiness required of us as that which is suited unto the holiness of God himself,—as that which it is meet for him to require, on the account of his own nature, and the infinite perfections thereof. The rule is, "Be ye holy, for I the LORD your God am holy;"—"I require that of you which becomes and answers my own holiness; because I am holy, it is necessary that you should be so; if you are mine in a peculiar manner, your holiness is that which becomes my holiness to require." We have before declared what this gospel holiness is, wherein it does consist, and what is required thereunto;—and they may be all considered either as they are in us, inherent in us, and performed by us; or as they are in themselves, in their own nature, and in the will of God. In the first way, I acknowledge that, by reason of our weaknesses, imperfections, and partial renovation only, as to degrees, in this life, with our manifold defects and sins, they make not a clear representation of the holiness of God; however, they are the best image of it, even as in the meanest of believers, that this world can afford. But in themselves, and their own nature, as it lies in the will of God, they make up the most glorious representation of himself that God ever did or will grant in this world; especially if we comprise therein the exemplification of it in the human nature of Christ himself: for the holiness that is in believers is of the same nature and kind with that which was and is in Jesus Christ, though his exceed theirs inconceivably in degrees of perfection.

Wherefore we are required to be holy, as the Lord our God is holy; and perfect, as our heavenly Father is perfect: which we could not be, but that in our holiness and perfection there is a resemblance and answerableness unto the holiness and perfection of God. And if a due sense hereof were continually upon our hearts, it would influence us unto greater care and diligence in all instances of duty and sin than, for the most part, we do attain unto and preserve. If we did on all occasions sincerely and severely call ourselves to an account whether our frames, ways, and actions bear a due resemblance unto the holiness and perfections of God, it would be a spiritual preservative on all occasions.

Faith, I say, then, discerns the likeness of God in this holiness, and every part of it,—sees it as that which becomes him to require; and thereon approves of it, reverencing God in it all: and it does so in all the parts of it, in all that belongs unto it.

1. It does so principally in the inward form of it, which we before described,—in the new creature, the new nature, the reparation of the image of God that is in it: in the beauty hereof it continually beholds the likeness and glory of God. For it is created "kata Theon",—according unto God, after him, or in his image,—"in righteousness and true holiness," Eph. iv. 24.

"The new man is renewed after the image of him that created him," Col. iii. 10. When God first created all things, the heavens and the earth, with all that is contained in them, he left such footsteps and impressions of his infinite wisdom, goodness, and power, on them, that they might signify and declare his perfection,—his eternal power and Godhead; yet did he not, he is not said to have created them in his own image. And this was because they were only a passive representation of him in the light of others, and not in themselves; nor did they represent at all that wherein God will be principally glorified among his creatures,—namely, the universal rectitude of his nature in righteousness and holiness. But of man it is said, peculiarly and only, that he was made in the image and likeness of God: and this was because, in the rectitude of his nature, he represented the holiness and righteousness of God; which is the only use of an image. This was lost by sin. Man in his fallen condition does no more represent God; there is nothing in him that has any thing of the likeness or image of God in it; all is dead, dark, perverse, and confused. This new nature, whereof we speak, is created of God for this very end, that it may be a blessed image and representation of the holiness and righteousness of God. Hence it is called the "divine nature," whereof we are partakers, 2 Pet. i. 4. And he that cannot see a representation of God in it, has not the light of faith and life in him. Hereon, I say, faith does approve of the form and principle of this holiness, as the renovation of the image of God in us; it looks upon it as that which becomes God to bestow and require, and therefore that which has an incomparable excellency and desirableness in it. Yea, when the soul is ready to faint under an apprehension that it is not partaker of this holy nature, because of the power of sin in it and temptations on it, it knows not whether itself be born of God or no (as is the case with many);— yet where this faith is, it will discern the beauty and glory of the new creation in some measure, as that which bears the image of God; and thereon does it preserve in the soul a longing after it, or a further participation of it.

By this work or act of it does faith discover its sincerity; which is that which we inquire after. Whilst it has an eye open to behold the glory of God in the new creature, whilst it looks on it as that wherein there is a representation made of the holiness of God himself, as that which becomes him to require in us, and thereon approves of it as excellent and desirable, it will be an anchor unto the soul in its greatest storms; for this is a work beyond what a mere enlightened conscience can arise unto. That can approve or disapprove of all the acts and effects of obedience and disobedience, as unto their consequent; but to discern the spiritual nature of the new creature, as representing the holiness of God himself, and thereon constantly to approve of it, is the work [of faith] alone.

2. It does the same with respect unto the internal acts and effects of this new creature, or principle of new obedience. The first thing it produces in us is a frame of mind spiritual and heavenly; they that are after the Spirit are "spiritually-minded," Rom. viii. 5, 6. It looks on the opposite frame, namely, of being carnally-minded, as vile and loathsome; it consisting in a readiness and disposition of mind to actuate the lusts of the flesh. But this spiritual frame of mind, in a just constellation of all the graces of the Spirit, influencing, disposing, and making ready the soul for the exercise of them on all occasions, and in all duties of obedience,—this is the inward glory of the "King's daughter," which faith sees and approves of, as that which becomes God to require in us; whatever is contrary hereunto, as a sensual, carnal, worldly frame of mind, it looks on as vile and base, unworthy of God, or of those who design the enjoyment of him.

3. It does the same with respect unto all particular duties, internal and external, when they are enlivened and filled up with grace. In them consists our "walking worthy at God," Col. i. 10; 1 Thess. ii. 12, such a walk as is meet for God to accept; that whereby and wherein he is glorified. The contrary hereunto, in the neglect of the duties of holiness, or the performance of them without the due exercise of grace, faith looks on as unworthy of God, unworthy of our high and holy calling, unworthy of our profession, and therefore does constantly condemn and abhor.

All this, as we observed before, faith will continue to do constantly, under temptations and desertions. There are seasons wherein the soul may be very weak, as unto the powers, effects, and duties of this spiritual life; such the psalmist oftentimes complains of in his own case, and it is evident in the experience of most. Few there are who have not found, at one time or another, great weakness, decays, and much deadness in their spiritual condition. And sometimes true believers may be at a loss as unto any refreshing experience of it in its operations. They may not be able to determine in the contest whether sin or grace have the dominion in them. Yet even in all these seasons faith will keep up the soul unto a constant high approbation of this way of holiness and obedience, in its root and fruits, in its principle and effects, in its nature, disposition, and duties. For when they cannot see the beauty of these things in themselves, they can see it in the promises of the covenant, in the truth of the gospel, wherein it is declared, and in the effects of it in others.

And great advantage is to be obtained by the due exercise of faith herein. For,—

(1.) It will never suffer the heart to be at rest in any sinful way, or under any such spiritual decays as shall estrange it from the pursuit of this holiness. The sight, the conviction of its excellency, the approbation of it, as that which in us and our measure answers the holiness of God, will keep up the mind unto endeavours after it, will rebuke the soul in all its neglects of it; nor will it allow any quiet or peace within, without an endeavour after a comfortable assurance of it. That soul is desperately sick which has lost an abiding sense of the excellency of this holiness, in its answerableness unto the holiness and will of God. Fears and checks of conscience are the whole of its security against the worst of sins; and they are a guard not to be trusted unto in the room of the peace of God. This is one great difference between believers and those that have not faith. Fear of the consequent of sin, with an apprehension of some advantages which are to be obtained by a sober life and the profession of religion, do steer and regulate the minds of unbelievers, in all they do towards God or for eternity; but the minds of believers are influenced by a view of the glory of the image and likeness of God in that holiness, and all the parts of it, which they are called unto. This gives them love unto it, delight and complacency in it, enabling them to look upon it as its own reward. And without these affections none will ever abide in the ways of obedience unto the end.

(2.) Where faith is in this exercise, it will evidence itself, unto the relief of the soul, in all its darkness and temptations. The mind can never conclude that it wholly is without God and his grace, whilst it constantly approves of the holiness required of us. This is not of ourselves; by nature we are ignorant of it. This "life is hid with Christ in God," Col. iii. 3, where we can see nothing of it; hereon we are alienated from it, and do dislike it: "Alienated from the life of God through the ignorance that is in us," Eph.4:18. And most men live all their days in a contempt of the principal evidences and duties of this life of God, and of the principle of it, which they look on as a fable. Wherefore, the mind may have great satisfaction in a sight of the beauty and approbation of this holiness, as that which nothing can produce but sincere and saving faith.

Secondly, Faith approves of this way of holiness and obedience, as that which gives that rectitude and perfection unto our nature whereof it is capable in this world. It is the only rule and measure of them; and whatever is contrary thereunto is perverse, crooked, vile, and base. Some men think that their nature is capable of no other perfection but what consists in the satisfaction of their lusts; they know no other blessedness, nothing that is suitable to their desires, but the saving of nature, in the pursuit of its corrupt lusts and pleasures. So are they described by the apostle, Eph. iv. 19. The business of their lives is to make provision for the flesh, to fulfill it in the lusts thereof; they walk in the lusts of the flesh, "fulfilling" (so far as they are able) "the desires of the flesh and of the mind," Eph. ii. 3. They neither know nor understand what a hell of confusion, disorder, and base degeneracy from the original constitution, their minds are filled withal. This perfection is nothing but the next disposition unto hell; and it does manifest its own vileness unto every one who has the least ray of spiritual light. Some among the heathen placed the rectitude of nature in moral virtues and operations, according unto them; and this was the utmost that natural light could ever rise up unto: but the uncertainty and weakness hereof are discovered by the light of the gospel.

It is faith alone that discovers what is good for us, in us, and unto us, whilst we are in this world. It is in the renovation of the image of God in us,—in the change and transformation of our nature into his likeness,—in acting from a gracious principle of a divine life,— in duties and operations suited thereunto,—in the participation of the divine nature by the promises,—that the good, the perfection, the order, the present blessedness of our nature do consist. Hereby are the faculties of our souls exalted, elevated, and enabled to act primigenial powers, with respect unto God and our enjoyment of him; which is our utmost end and blessedness. Hereby are our affections placed on their proper objects (such as they were created meet for, and in closing wherewith their satisfaction, order, and rest do consist),— namely, God and his goodness, or God as revealed in Jesus Christ by the gospel. Hereby all the powers of our souls are brought into a blessed frame and harmony in all their operations,—whatever is dark, perverse, unquiet, vile, and base, being cast out of them. But these things must be a little more distinctly explained.

1. There is in this gospel holiness, as the spring and principle of it, a spiritual, saving light, enabling the mind and understanding to know God in Christ, and to discern spiritual things in a spiritual, saving manner; for herein "God shines into our hearts, to give us the knowledge of his glory in the face of Jesus Christ," 2 Cor. iv. 6. Without this, in some degree, whatever pretence there may be or appearance of holiness in any, there is nothing in them of what is really so, and thereon accepted with God. Blind devotion,— that is, an inclination of mind unto religious duties, destitute of this light,—will put men on a multiplication of duties, especially such as are of their own invention, in "a show of wisdom in will-worship, and humility, and neglecting of the body," as the apostle speaks, Col. ii. 23; wherein there is nothing of gospel holiness. "The new man is renewed in knowledge after the image of him that created him," Col. iii. 10. That this saving light and knowledge is the spring and principle of all real evangelical holiness and obedience, the apostle declares in that description which he gives us of the whole of it, both in its beginning and progress, Col. i. 9-11, "We desire that ye might be filled with the knowledge of his will, in all wisdom and spiritual understanding; that ye might walk worthy of the Lord unto all

pleasing, being fruitful in every good work, and increasing in the knowledge of God; strengthened with all might, according to his glorious power, unto all patience and long suffering with joyfulness." It is a blessed account that is here given us of that gospel holiness which we inquire after, in its nature, original, spring, progress, fruits, and effects; and a serious consideration of it as here proposed,—a view of it in the light of faith,—will evidence how distant and different it is from those schemes of moral virtues which some would substitute in its room. It has a glory in it which no unenlightened mind can behold or comprehend; the foundation of it is laid in the knowledge of the will of God, in all wisdom and spiritual understanding. This is that spiritual, saving light whereof we speak; the increase hereof is prayed for in believers by the apostle, Heb. i. 17, 18, even "that the God of our Lord Jesus Christ, the Father of glory, would give unto you the spirit of wisdom and revelation in the knowledge of him: the eyes of your understanding being enlightened; that ye may know what is the hope of his calling, and what the riches of the glory of his inheritance in the saints;" which here is called "increasing in the knowledge of God," verse 10. The singular glory of this saving light, in its original, its causes, use, and effects, is most illustriously here declared: and this light is in every true believer, and is the only immediate spring of all gospel holiness and obedience; for "the new man is renewed in knowledge after the image of him that created him," Col. iii. 10.

This light, this wisdom, this spiritual understanding, thus communicated unto believers, is the rectitude and perfection of their minds in this world. It is that which gives them order, and peace, and power, enabling them to act all their faculties in a due manner, with respect unto their being and end. It is that which gives beauty and glory to the inward man, and which constitutes a believer an inhabitant of the kingdom of light,— whereby we are "delivered from the power of darkness, and translated into the kingdom of the Son of God's love," Col. i. 13; or "out of darkness into his marvellous light," 1 Pet. ii. 9. That which is contrary hereunto, is that ignorance, darkness, blindness, and vanity, which the Scripture declares to be in the minds of all unregenerate persons; and they are really so, where they are not cured by the glorious working of the power and grace of God before mentioned. Now, faith discerns these things, as the spiritual man discerns all things, I Cor. ii. 15. It sees the beauty of this heavenly light, and judges that it is that which gives order and rectitude unto the mind; as also, that that which is contrary unto it is vile, base, horrid, and to be ashamed of. As for those who "love darkness more than light, because their deeds are evil,"—it knows them to be strangers unto Christ and his gospel.

2. Again: there is required unto this holiness, a principle of spiritual life and love unto God. This guides, acts, and rules in the soul, in all its obedience; and it gives the soul its proper order in all its operations: that which is contrary hereunto is death, and enmity against God. Faith judges between these two principles and their operations: the former in all its acting it approves of as lovely, beautiful, desirable, as that which is the rectitude and perfection of the will: and the other it looks on as deformed, froward, and perverse.

3. The like may be said of its nature and operations in the affections, as also of all those duties of obedience which proceed from it, as it is described in the place before mentioned. It remains only that we show by what acts, ways, and means, faith does evidence this its approbation of gospel holiness, as that which is lovely and desirable in itself, and which gives all that rectitude and perfection unto our minds which they are capable of in this world. And it does so,—

1. By that self-discipline and abasement which it works in the mind on all instances and occasions where it comes short of this holiness. This is the chief principle and cause of that holy shame which befalls believers on every sin and miscarriage, wherein they come short of what is required in it: Rom. vi. 21, "Those things whereof ye are now ashamed." Now when, by the light of

faith, you see how vile it is, and unworthy of you, what a debasement of your souls there is in it, you are ashamed of it. It is true, the principal cause of this holy shame is a sense of the unsuitableness that is in sin unto the holiness of God, and the horrible ingratitude and disingenuity that there is in sinning against him; but it is greatly promoted by this consideration, that it is a thing unworthy of us, and that wherein our natures are exceedingly debased. So it is said of provoking sinners, that they "debase themselves even unto hell," Isa. lvii. 9; or make themselves as vile as hell itself, by ways unworthy the nature of men. And this is one ground of all those severe self reflections which accompany godly sorrow for sin, 2 Cor. vii. 11. And hereby does faith evidence itself and its own sincerity, whilst a man is ashamed of, and abased in, himself for every sin, for every thing of sin, wherein it comes short of the holiness required of us, as that which is base and unworthy of our nature, in its present constitution and renovation; though it be that which no eye sees but God's and his own, he has that in him which will grow on no root but sincere believing. Wherefore, whatever may be the disquieting conflicts of sin in and against our souls, whatever decays we may fall into,—which be the two principles of darkness and fears in believers, whilst this inward holy shame and self- abasement, on account of the vileness of sin, is preserved, faith leaves not itself without an evidence in us.

2. It does the same by a spiritual satisfaction, which it gives the soul in every experience of the transforming power of this holiness, rendering it more and more like unto God. There is a secret joy and spiritual refreshment rising in the soul from a sense of its renovation into the image of God; and all the acting and increases of the life of God in it augment this joy. Herein consists its gradual return unto its primitive order and rectitude, with a blessed addition of supernatural light and grace by Christ Jesus; it finds itself herein coming home to God from its old apostasy, in the way of approaching to eternal rest and blessedness: and there is no satisfaction like unto that which it receives therein.

This is the second way wherein faith will abide firm and constant, and does evidence itself in the soul of every believer. However low and mean its attainments be in this spiritual life and the fruits of it, though it be overwhelmed with darkness and a sense of the guilt of sin, though it be surprised and perplexed with the deceit and violence thereof, yet faith will continue here firm and unshaken. It sees that glory and excellency in the holiness and obedience that God requires of us,—as it is a representation of his own glorious excellencies, the renovation of his image, and the perfection of our natures thereby,—as that it constantly approves of it, even in the deepest trials which the soul can be exercised withal; and whilst this anchor holds firm and stable we are safe.

III

The third evidence of the faith of God's elect

THIRDLY, Faith will evidence itself by a diligent, constant endeavour to keep itself and all grace in due exercise in all ordinances of divine worship, private and public.

This is the touchstone of faith and spiritual obedience, the most intimate and difficult part of this exercise; where this is not, there is no life in the soul. There are two things whereby men do or may deceive themselves herein:—

1. Abounding in the outward performance of duties or a multiplication of them. Hereby hypocrites have in all ages deceived themselves, Isa. lviii. 2, 3. And it was the covering that the church of Rome provided for their apostasy from the gospel: an endless multiplication of religious duties was that which they trusted to and boasted in. And we may find those daily that pretend a conscience as unto the constant observation of outward duties, and yet will abstain from no sin that comes in the way of their lusts. And men may and do ofttimes abide constantly in them, especially in their families and in public, yea, multiply them beyond the ordinary measure, hoping to countenance themselves in other lusts and neglects thereby.

2. Assistance of gifts in the performance of them; but as this may be where there is not one dram of grace, saving grace, so when rested in, it is a most powerful engine to keep the soul in formality, to ruin all beginning of grace, and to bring an incurable hardness on the whole soul. Wherever faith is in sincerity, it will constantly labour, endeavour, and strive to fill up all duties of divine worship with the living, real, heart acting of grace; and where it does not so, where this is not attained, it will never suffer the soul to take any rest or satisfaction in such duties, but will cast them away as a defiled garment. He that can pass through such duties without a sensible endeavour for the real exercise of grace in them, and without self-abasement on the performance of them, will hardly find any other clear evidence of saving faith in himself. There are three evils that have followed the ignorance, or neglect, or weariness of this exercise of faith, which have proved the ruin of multitudes:—

1. This has been the occasion and original of all false worship in the world, with the invention of those superstitious rites and ceremonies wherein it consists. For men having lost the exercise of faith in the ordinances of worship that are of divine institution, they found the whole of it to be useless and burdensome unto them; for without this constant exercise of faith there is no life in it, nor satisfaction to be obtained by it. They must, therefore, have something in it, or

accompanying of it, which may entertain their minds, and engage their affections unto it. If this had not been done, it would have been utterly deserted by the most. Hereon were invented forms of prayer in great diversity, with continual diversions and avocations of the mind from what is proposed; because it cannot abide in the pursuit of any thing spiritual without the exercise of faith. This gives it some entertainment by the mere performance, and makes it think there is something where indeed is nothing. Hereunto are added outward ceremonies of vestments, postures, and gestures of veneration, unto the same end. There is no other design in them all but to entertain the mind and affections with some complacency and satisfaction in outward worship, upon the loss or want of that exercise of faith which is the life and soul of it in believers. And as any persons do decay herein, they shall find themselves insensibly sinking down into the use of these lifeless forms, or that exercise of their natural faculties and memory which is not one jot better; yea, by this means, some, from an eminency in spiritual gifts, and the performance of duties by virtue of them, have sunk into an Ave Maria or a Credo, as the best of their devotion.

2. This has caused many to turn aside, to fall off from and forsake the solemn ordinances of divine worship, and to retake themselves unto vain imaginations for relief, in trembling, enthusiastical singing and feigned raptures; from

hence have so many forsaken their own mercies to follow after lying vanities. They kept for a while unto the observance of the divine institutions of worship; but not having faith to exercise in them, by which alone they are life and power, they became useless and burdensome unto them: they could find neither sweetness, satisfaction, nor benefit in them. It is not possible that so many in our days, if ever they had tasted of the old wine, should so go after new;—if ever they had experience of that savour, power, and life, which is in the ordinances of divine worship, when acted and enlivened by the exercise of faith, should forsake them for that which is nothing: "They went out from us, but they were not of us; for if they had been of us, they would have continued with us." "Had they known it, they would not have crucified the Lord of glory." This, therefore, is the true reason why so many in our days, after they have for a season abode under, and in the observation of, the gospel ordinances of worship, have fallen off from them, namely, not having faith to exercise in them, nor endeavouring after it, they did really find no life in them, nor benefit by them.

3. Some, on the same ground, fall into profaneness, pretending to take up with a natural religion, without any instituted worship at all. Of this sort of persons we have multitudes in the days wherein we live; having nothing of the light of faith, they can see no form or comeliness in Christ, nor in any thing that belongs unto him. By

these means are souls every day precipitated into ruin.

Herein, therefore, I say, true faith will evidence itself in all darknesses and distress whatsoever: it will always endeavour to keep itself, and all other graces, in a due and constant exercise in all duties of worship, private and public. It may sometimes be weakened in its acting and operations, it may be under decays, it may be as a sleep, and that not only as unto particular duties and seasons, but as unto the inward habitual frame of the mind; but where it is true and genuine, it will shake itself out of this dust, cast off the sin that does so easily beset us, and stir up itself, with all might and contention, unto its duty. And there is no more dangerous state for a soul than when it is sinking down into formality, and neglect of the exercise of faith, in a multitude of duties; then is it assuredly ready to die, if it be not dead already. If we are wise, therefore, we will watch, and take care that we lose not this evidence of faith; it will stand us instead when, it may be, all other things seem to be against us. Some have been relieved by the remembrance of this exercise of faith, when they have been at the door of desperation:—such or such a season they had experience of the work of faith in prayer, has been their relief. An experience hereof is a jewel, which may be of no great use whilst it lies by you locked up in a cabinet, but which you will know the worth of if ever you come to need bread for your lives.

It is, therefore, worthwhile to inquire what we ought to do, or what means we ought to use, that we may keep up faith unto its due exercise in all the parts of divine worship, so as that it may give us a comforting evidence of itself in times of temptation and darkness? And unto this end the ensuing directions may be of use:—

1. Labour to have your hearts always affected with a due sense of the infinite perfections of the divine nature in all our approaches unto him, especially of his sovereign power, holiness, immensity, and omnipresence; and this will produce in us also a sense of infinite distance from him. As this is necessary, from the nature of the things themselves, so the Scripture gives us such descriptions of God as are suited to in generate this frame in us. This is that which Joshua aimed to bring the people unto, when he designed to engage them in the service of God in a due manner, Josh. xxiv. 19-22; and that which the apostle requires in us, Heb. xii. 28, 29. And unto the same end glorious descriptions and appearances of God are multiplied in Scripture. If we fail herein, if we do not on all occasions fill our minds with reverential thoughts of God, his greatness and his holiness, faith has no foundation to stand upon in its exercise in the duties of worship. This is the only inlet into the due exercise of grace: where it is wanting, all holy thoughts and affections are shut out of our minds; and where it is present, it is impossible but

that there will be some gracious working of heart in all our duties. If we are empty hereof in our entrance of duties, we shall be sure to be filled with other things, which will be clogs and hindrances unto us; but reverential thoughts of God, in our approaches unto him, will cast out all superfluity of naughtiness, and dissipate all carnal, formal frames, which will vitiate all our duties. Keep your hearts, therefore, under this charge in all your accesses unto God, and it will constantly open a door unto that exercise of faith which we inquire after. Hereon and herewith we shall be affected with a sense of our infinite distance from him; which is another means to stir up faith unto its due exercise in reverence and godly fear. So Abraham was affected, Gen. xviii. 27. [This is that] which the wise man directs us unto, Eccles. v. 2. Carnal boldness in the want of these things ruins the souls of men, rendering all their duties of worship unacceptable unto God, and unprofitable unto themselves.

2. Affect your hearts with a due sense of the unsuitableness of our best duties unto his holiness and majesty, and of his infinite condescension in the acceptance of them. Suppose there is in any of our duties the best and the most lively exercise of grace that we can attain unto, the most fervency in prayer, with the most diligent attendance of our minds the most humility and contrite trembling in hearing the word, the most devout affection of our minds in other parts of worship; alas! what is all this to

God? How little does it answer his infinite holiness! See Job iv. 18 ,19; xv. 15, 16. Our goodness extends not unto him, Ps. xvi. 2. There are no measures, there is no proportion, between the holiness of God and our best duties. There is iniquity in our holy things; they have need of mercy and pardon, of cleansing and justification, by the blood of Christ, no less than our persons: and an infinite condescension it is in God to take any notice of us or them; yea, it is that which we must live in all holy admiration of all our days.

Now if it be thus with our best duties, in our best frames, what an outrage of sloth and negligence is it, if we bring the carcass of duties unto God, for want of stirring up faith unto its due exercise in them! How great is this folly, how unspeakable is the guilt of this negligence! Let us, therefore, keep a sense hereof upon our hearts, that we may always stir up ourselves unto our best in duties of religious worship. For,—

3. A negligence herein, or the want of stirring up faith unto a due exercise in all duties of worship, is the highest affront we can put upon God, arguing a great regardlessness of him. Whilst it is so with us, we have not, we cannot have, a due sense of any of the divine perfections, of the divine nature; we turn God what lies in us into an idol, supposing that he may be put off with the outside and appearance of things. This the apostle cautions us against, Heb. iv. 12, 13, and [is that] which God detests, Isa. xxix. 13; and

he pronounces him a deceiver, and cursed, who offers unto him the lame and blind while he has a male in the flock, Mal. i. 14. Yet thus is it with us, in some degree, whenever we are negligent in stirring up faith into its proper exercise in holy duties: that alone renders them the male of the flock; without it they are lame and blind,—a corrupt thing.

It is a sad thing for men to lose their duties, to be at charge and trouble in the multiplication of them, and attendance unto them to no purpose. Oh, how much more sad is it when they are all provocations of God's glory! when they tend to increase the formality and hardness of their hearts, towards the ruin of their souls!

"Stand in awe," therefore, "and sin not; commune with your own hearts;" cease not, until on all occasions you bring them into that exercise of faith wherein you may glorify God as God, and not deal with him as an idol.

4. Unto the same end, keep your souls always deeply affected with a sense of the things about which you are to treat with God in all the duties of his worship. They are referred unto two heads:—

(1.) Those which concern his glory; (2.) Those which concern our own souls. Without a constant due sense of these things on our hearts, faith will not act itself aright in any of our duties. Without this intimate concern and deep sense, we know not whether we need faith in our prayers, or have an exercise of it; formality will drown all. The best of our prayers is but an expression unto God of what sense we have of these things. If we have none, we pray not at all, whatever we say or do; but when these things dwell in our minds, when we think on them continually, when our hearts cleave unto them, faith will be at work in all our approaches to God. Can you not pray? Charge your hearts with these things, and you will learn so to do.

5. Watch diligently against those things which ye find by experience are apt to obstruct your fervency in duties. Such are indispositions through the flesh, or weariness of the flesh, distracting, foolish imaginations, the occasions of life revolving in our minds, and the like. If such impediments as these be not removed, if they be not watched against, they will influence the mind, and suffocate the exercise of faith therein.

6. Above all, the principal rule herein is, that we would always carefully remember the concernment of Christ in these duties, with respect unto his office. He is the high priest over the house of God; through him, and under his conduct, are we always to draw nigh to God; and his work it is to present the prayers and supplications of the church to God. Now, we have no way to come unto Christ, for his assistance in the discharge of his office on our behalf, but by faith; and in all our duties of holy worship we make a profession of our doing so,—

of our coming unto God by him as our high priest. If we endeavour not therein to have faith in exercise, how do we mock, or make a show to him of doing that which indeed we endeavour not to do! There can be no greater contempt of Christ in his office, nor greater undervaluation of his love. But a due consideration hereof, namely, of the concernment of Christ in all our duties, with respect unto the office which he discharges for us in heaven,—is that which directly leads faith into its proper exercise. For through him, and that in discharge of his office, we believe in God. And when the mind is exercised with due thoughts of him, if there be any thing of true saving faith in the heart, it will act itself unto a blessed experience.

These things may be of use to stir us up, and guide us unto that exercise of faith in all holy duties, an experience whereof abiding in the soul will evidence the truth of it, unto our supportment and comfort in all temptations and distresses.

Some, it may be, will say that their gift in prayer is mean and weak,—that they cannot express themselves with earnestness and fervency; and so know not whether there be any faith in exercise in their prayers or no. I answer, There is nothing at all herein; for grace may be very high where gifts are very low, and that frequently.

And it may be others will complain of the meanness of their gifts on whom they attend in prayer, which is such as they cannot accompany them in the exercise of any grace. I answer,—

1. There is no doubt but that there is a great difference in the spiritual gifts of men in this matter, some being much more effectual unto edification than others.

2. Take care that you are called in providence and duty to join with them whom you intend; that you do not first voluntarily choose that which is unto your disadvantage, and then complain of it. 3. Be their gifts never so mean, if grace in their own hearts be exercised by it, so it may be in ours: where there is no evidence thereof, I confess the case is hard. 4. Let the mind be still fixed on the matter or things uttered in prayer, so as to close with, and act faith about, what is real object of it, and it will find its proper work in that duty.

IV

The fourth evidence of the faith of God's elect

I COME, in the next place, to instance in a peculiar way whereby true faith will evidence itself,—not always, but on some occasions: and this is by bringing the soul into a state of repentance. And three things must be spoken unto,— 1. In general, what I intend by this state of repentance. 2. What are the times and occasions, or who are the persons, wherein faith will act itself unto this end. 3. What are the duties required unto such a state.

1. By this state of repentance I do not understand merely the grace and duty of evangelical repentance; for this is absolutely inseparable from true faith, and no less necessary unto salvation than itself. He that does not truly and really repent of sin, whatever he profess himself to believe, he is no true believer. But I intend now somewhat that is peculiar, that is not common unto all, whereby on some occasions faith does evidence its power and sincerity.

Neither yet do I mean a grace, duty, or state, that is of another kind or nature from that of gospel repentance, which is common to all believers. There are not two kinds of true repentance, nor two different states of them that are truly penitent; all that I intend is an eminent degree of gospel repentance, in the habit or root, and in all the fruits and effects of it. There are various degrees in the power and exercise of gospel graces, and some may be more eminent in one, and some in another: as Abraham and Peter in faith, David and John in love. And there may be causes and occasions for the greater and higher exercise of some graces and duties at one time than at another; for we are to attend unto duties according unto our circumstances, so as we may glorify God in them, and advantage our own souls. So the apostle James directs us, chap.5:13, "Is any afflicted? Let him pray. Is any merry? Let him sing psalms." Several states, and various circumstances in them, call for the peculiar exercise of several graces, and the diligent performance of several duties. And this is that which is here intended,—namely, a peculiar, constant, prevalent exercise of the grace and duties of repentance in a singular manner. What is required hereunto shall be afterwards declared.

2. As unto the persons in whom this is required, and in whom faith will evidence itself by it, they are of various sorts:—

(1.) Such as have been, by the power of their corruptions and temptations, surprised into great sins. That some true believers may be so, we have precedents both in the Old Testament and in the New;— such, I mean, as uncleanness, drunkenness, gluttony, theft, premeditated lying, oppression in dealing, and failing in profession in the time of persecution; this latter in the primitive church was never thought recoverable but by faith acting itself in a state of repentance. Such sins will have great sorrows; as we see in Peter, and the incestuous Corinthian, who was in danger to be "swallowed up with overmuch sorrow," 2 Cor. ii. 7. Where it has been thus with any, true faith will immediately work for a recovery, by a thorough humiliation and repentance, as it did in Peter; and in case that any of them shall lie longer under the power of sin, through want of effectual convictions, it will cost them dear in the issue, as it did David. But in this case, for the most part, faith will not rest in the mere jointing again the bone that was broken, or with such a recovery as gives them peace with God and their own consciences; but by a just and due remembrance of the nature of their sin, its circumstances and aggravations, the shameful unkindness towards God that was in it, the grief of the Holy Spirit, and dishonour of Christ by it, it will incline and dispose the soul to a humble, contrite frame, to a mournful walking, and the universal exercise of repentance all its days.

And, indeed, where it does not so, men's recovery from great sins is justly to be questioned as unto their sincerity. For want hereof it is that we have so many palliated cures of great sins, followed with fearful and dangerous relapses. If a man subject to great corruptions and temptations, has by them been surprised into great actual sins, and been seemingly recovered through humiliation and repentance, if he again break the yoke of this stated repentance whereof we speak, he will quickly again be overcome, and perhaps irrecoverably. Herein, he alone that walks softly, walks safely.

(2.) It is necessary for such as have given scandal and offence by their miscarriages; this will stick very close unto any who has the least spark of saving faith. It is that which God is in a peculiar manner provoked with in the sins of his people; as in the case of David, 2 Sam. xii. 14. So also Ezek. xxxvi. 20; Rom. ii. 24. This keeps alive the remembrance of sin, and sets it before men continually, and is a spring, in a gracious soul, of all acts and duties of repentance. It was so in David all his days; and probably in Mary Magdalene also. Where it has been thus with any, faith will keep the soul in an humble and contrite frame, watchful against pride, elation of mind, carelessness, and sloth: it will recover godly sorrow and shame, with revenge, or self-reflection, in great abasement of mind; all which things belong to the state of repentance intended. They that can easily shake off a sense of scandal given by them, have very little of Christian ingenuity in their minds.

(3.) It is so unto such as have perplexing lusts and corruptions, which they cannot so subdue but that they will be perplexing and defiling of them; for where there are such, they will, in conjunction with temptations, frequently disquiet, wound, and defile the soul. This brings upon it weariness and outcries for deliverance, Rom. vii. 24. In this state faith will put the soul on prayer, watchfulness, diligence, in opposition unto the deceit and violence of sin. But this is not all; it will not rest here, but it will give the mind such a sense of its distressed, dangerous condition, as shall fill it constantly with godly sorrow, self-abasement, and all duties of repentance. No man can hold out in such a conflict, nor maintain his peace on right grounds, who does not live in the constant exercise of repentance,—indeed, who does not endeavour in some measure to come up unto that state of it which we shall afterwards describe. For men who have unnameable corruptions working continually in their minds, by imaginations, thoughts, and affections, to think to carry it in a general way of duties and profession, they will be mistaken if they look either for victory or peace; this sort of men are, of all others, most peculiarly called unto this state and duty.

(4.) Such as would be found mourners for the sins of the age, place, and time wherein they live, with the consequent of them, in the dishonour of God, and the judgments which will ensue thereon. There are times wherein this is an especial and eminent duty, which God does highly approve of. Such are they wherein the visible church is greatly corrupted, and open abominations are found amongst men of all sorts; even as it is at this day. Then does the Lord declare how much he values the performance of this duty,—as he testifies, Ezek. ix. 4, they alone shall be under his especial care in a day of public distress and calamity,—a duty wherein it is to be feared that we are most of us very defective. Now, the frame of heart required hereunto cannot be attained, nor the duty rightly performed, without that state of repentance and humiliation which we inquire into. Without it we may have transient thoughts of these things, but such as will very little affect our minds; but where the soul is kept in a constant spiritual frame, it will be ready for this duty on all occasions.

(5.) It becomes them who, having passed through the greatest part of their lives, do find all outward things to issue in vanity and vexation of spirit, as it was with Solomon when he wrote his Ecclesiastes. When a man recounts the various scenes and appearances of things which he has passed through in his life, and the various conditions he has been in, he may possibly find that there is nothing steady but sorrow and trouble. It may be so with some, I say, with some good men, with some of the best men, as it was with Jacob. Others may have received more satisfaction in their course; but if they also will look back, they shall find how little there has been in the best of their transient comforts; they will see enough to make them say, "There is nothing in these things; it is high time to take off all expectations from them." Such persons seem to be called unto this especial exercise of repentance and mourning for the remainder of their lives.

(6.) Such as whose hearts are really wounded and deeply affected with the love of Christ, so as that they can hardly bear any longer absence from him, nor delight in the things wherein they are detained and kept out of his presence. This frame the apostle describes, 2 Cor. v. 2, 4, 6, 8. They live in a groaning condition, thoroughly sensible of all the evils that accompany them in this absence of the Bridegroom; and they cannot but continually reflect upon the sins and follies which their lives have been and are filled withal, in this their distance from Christ. Whereas, therefore, their hearts are filled with inflamed affections towards him, they cannot but walk humbly and mournfully until they come unto him. It may be said that those who have experience of such affection unto the Lord Jesus cannot but have continual matter of joy in themselves; and so of all men have least need of such a state of constant humiliation and repentance. I say it is so indeed, they have such matter of joy; and therewith Christ will be formed in them more and more every day. But I say also, there is no inconsistency between spiritual joy in Christ and godly sorrow for sin; yea, no man in this life shall ever be able to maintain solid joy in his heart, without the continual working of godly sorrow also; yea, there is a secret joy and refreshment in godly sorrow, equal unto the chiefest of our joys, and a great spiritual satisfaction. These several sorts of persons, I say, are peculiarly called unto that exercise of faith in repentance which we inquire after.

Before I proceed to show wherein this state I intend does consist, and what is required thereunto (which is the last thing proposed), I shall premise some rules for the right judging of ourselves with respect unto them As,—

1. Faith will evidence its truth (which is that we inquire after) in its sincere endeavour after the things intended, though its attainments as unto some of them be but mean and low, yea, a sense of its corning short in a full answering of them or compliance with them, is a great ingredient in that state called unto. If, therefore, faith keep up this design in the soul, with a sincere pursuit of it, though it fail in many things, and is not sensible of any great progress it makes, it will therein evidence its sincerity.

2. Whereas there are sundry things, as we shall see, required hereunto, it is not necessary that they should be found all equally in all who design this state and frame. Some may be more eminent in one of them, some in another; some may have great helps and furtherance unto some of them in a peculiar manner, and some great obstructions in the exercise of some of them. But it is required that they be all radically in the heart, and be put forth in exercise sometimes, on their proper occasions.

3. This state, in the description of it, will sufficiently distinguish itself from that discontent of mind whereon some withdraw themselves from the occasions of life, rather condemning others than themselves, on mere weariness of the disappointments of the world, which has cast some into crooked paths.

1. The first thing required hereunto is weanedness from the world. The rule of most men is, that all things are well enough with them, with respect unto the world, whilst they keep themselves from known particular sins in the use of the things of it. Whilst they do so in their own apprehensions, they care not how much they cleave unto it,—are even swallowed up in the businesses and occasions of it. Yea, some will pretend unto and make an appearance of a course of life more than ordinarily strict, whilst their hearts and affections cleave visibly to this world and the things of it. But the foundation of the work of faith we inquire into must be laid in mortification and weanedness from the world. In ancient times, sundry persons designed a strict course of mortification and penitence, and they always laid the foundation of it in a renunciation of the world; but they fell most of them into a threefold mistake, which ruined the whole undertaking. For,—

(1.) They fell into a neglect of such natural and moral duties as were indispensably required of them: they forsook all care of duties belonging unto them in their relations as fathers, children, husbands, wives, and the like, retaking themselves into solitudes; and hereby also they lost all that political and Christian usefulness which the principles of human society and of our religion do oblige us unto. They took themselves unto a course of life rendering the most important Christian duties, such as respect other men of all sorts, in all fruits of love, utterly impossible unto them. They could be no more useful nor helpful in the places and circumstances wherein they were set by divine Providence: which was a way wherein they could not expect any blessing from God. No such thing is required unto that renunciation of the world which we design; with nothing that should render men useless unto all men do Christian duties interfere. We are still to use the world whilst we are in it, but not abuse it; as we have opportunity, we must still do good unto all. Yea, none will be so ready to the duties of life as those who are most mortified to the world. Thoughts of retirement from usefulness, unless [under] a great decay of outward strength, are but temptations.

(2.) They engaged themselves into a number of observances nowhere required of them: such were their outward austerities, fastings, choice of meats, times of prayer; whereunto, at length, self-maceration and disciplines were added. In a scrupulous, superstitious observance of these things their whole design at length issued, giving rise and occasion unto innumerable evils. Faith directs to no such thing; it guides to no duty but according to the rule of the word.

(3.) At length they began to engage themselves by vow into such peculiar orders and rules of a pretended religious life as were by some of their leaders presented unto them; and this ruined the whole. However, the original design was good,— namely, such a renunciation of the world as might keep it and all the things of it from being a hindrance unto us in an humble walk before God, or any thing that belongs thereunto. We are to be crucified unto the world, and the world unto us, by the cross of Christ; we are to be so in a peculiar manner, if we are under the conduct of faith, in a way of humiliation and repentance. And the things ensuing are required hereunto:—

(1.) The mortification of our affections unto the desirable things of this life: they are naturally keen and sharp-set upon them, and do tenaciously adhere unto them; especially they are so when things have an inlet into them by nearness of relation, as husbands, wives, children, and the like. Persons are apt to think they can never love them enough, never do enough for them (and it is granted they are to be preferred above all other earthly things); but where they fill and possess the heart, where they weaken and obtund the affections unto things spiritual, heavenly, and eternal, unless we are mortified unto them, the heart will never be in a good frame, nor is capable of that degree in the grace of repentance which we seek. It is so with the most, as unto all other useful things in this world,—as wealth, estates, and peace: whilst they are conversant about them, as they suppose in a lawful manner, they think they can never overvalue them, nor cleave too close unto them. But here we must begin, if we intend to take any one step into this holy retirement. The edge of our affections and desires must be taken off from these things: and hereunto three things are necessary:—

[1.] constant, clear view and judgment of their uncertainty, emptiness, and disability to give any rest or satisfaction. Uncertain riches, uncertain enjoyments, perishing things, passing away, yea, snares, burdens, hindrances, the Scripture represents them to be;—and so they are. If the mind were continually charged home with this consideration of them, it would daily abate its delight and satisfaction in them.

[2.] A constant endeavour for conformity unto Christ crucified. It is the cross of Christ whereby we are crucified unto the world and all things in it. When the mind is much taken up with thoughts of Christ, as dying, how and for what he died, if it has any spark of saving faith in it, it will turn away the eyes from looking on the desirable things of this world with any delightful, friendly aspect. Things will appear unto it as dead and discoloured.

[3.] The fixing of them steadily on things spiritual and eternal; whereof I have discoursed at large elsewhere. The whole of this advice is given us by the apostle, Col. iii. 1-5.

Herein faith begins its work, this is the first lesson it takes out of the gospel,—namely, that of self-denial, whereof this mortification is a principal part. Herein it labours to cast off every burden, and the sin that does so easily beset us. Unless some good degree be attained here, all further attempts in this great duty will be fruitless. Do you, then, any of you, judge yourselves under any of those qualifications before mentioned, which render this duty and work of faith necessary unto you? Sit down here at the threshold, and reckon with yourselves that unless you can take your hearts more off from the world,— unless your affections and desires be mortified and crucified, and dead in you, in a sensible degree and measure,—unless you endeavour every day to promote the same frame in your minds,— you will live and die strangers to this duty.

(2.) This mortification of our affections towards these things, our love, desire, and delight, will produce a moderation of passions about them, as fear, anger, sorrow, and the like; such will men be stirred up unto in those changes, losses, crosses, which these things are subject unto. They are apt to be tender and soft in those things; they take every thing to heart; every affliction and disappointment is aggravated, as if none almost had such things befall them as themselves; every thing puts them into a commotion. Hence are they often surprised with anger about trifles, influenced by fear in all changes, with other turbulent passions. Hence are men morose, peevish, froward, apt to be displeased and take offence on all occasions. The subduing of this frame, the casting out of these dispositions and perverse inclinations, is part of the work of faith. When the mind is weaned from the world and the things of it, it will be sedate, quiet, composed, not easily moved with the occurrences and occasions of life: it is dead unto them, and in a great measure unconcerned in them. This is that "moderation" of mind wherein the apostle would have us excel, Phil. iv. 5; for he would have it so eminent as that it might appear unto "all men," that is, who are concerned in us, as relations, families, and other societies. This is that which principally renders us useful and exemplary in this world; and for the want whereof many professors fill themselves and others with disquietments, and give offence unto the world itself. This is required of all believers; but they will be eminent in it in whom faith works this weanedness from the world, in order unto a peculiar exercise of repentance.

(3.) There is required hereunto an unsolicitousness about present affairs and future events. There is nothing given us in more strict charge in the Scripture, than that we should be careful in nothing, solicitous about nothing, take no thought for tomorrow, but to commit all things unto the sovereign disposal of our God and Father, who has taken all these things into his own care. But so it is come to pass, through the vanity of the minds of men, that what should be nothing unto them is almost their all. Care about things present, and solicitousness about things to come, in private and public concerns, take up most of their thoughts and contrivances. But this also will faith subdue on this occasion, where it tends unto the promotion of repentance, by weanedness from the world. It will bring the soul into a constant, steady, universal resignation of itself unto the pleasure of God, and satisfaction in his will. Hereon it will use the world as if it used it not, with an absolute unconcernment in it as unto what shall fall out. This is that which our Saviour presses so at large, and with so many divine seasonings, Matt vi. 25-34.

(4.) A constant preference of the duties of religion before and above the duties and occasions of life. These things will continually interfere if a diligent watch be not kept over them, and they will contend for preference; and their success is according to the interest and estimation which the things themselves have in our minds. If the interest of the world be there prevalent, the occasions of it will be preferred before religious duties; and they shall, for the most part, be put off unto such seasons wherein we have nothing else to do, and it may be fit for little else. But where the interest of spiritual things prevail it will be otherwise, according to the rule given us by our blessed Saviour, "Seek first the kingdom of God and the righteousness thereof," etc., Matt. vi. 33.

I confess this rule is not absolute as unto all seasons and occasions: there may be a time wherein the observation of the Sabbath must give place to the pulling an ox or an ass out of a pit; and on all such occasions the rule is, that mercy is to be preferred before sacrifice. But, in the ordinary course of our walking before God, faith will take care that a due attendance unto all duties of religion be preferred to all the occasions of this life; they shall not be shuffled off on trifling pretences, nor cast into such unseasonable seasons as otherwise they will be. There also belongs unto that weanedness from this world, which is necessary unto an eminency in degrees of humiliation and repentance, watching unto prayer.

(5.) Willingness and readiness to part with all for Christ and the gospel. This is the animating principle of the great duty of taking up the cross, and self-denial therein. Without some measure of it in sincerity, we cannot be Christ's disciples; but in the present case there is an eminent degree, which Christ calls the hating of all things in comparison of him, that is required,—such a readiness as rejects with contempt all arguing against it,—such as renders the world no burden unto it in any part of our race,—such as establishes a determinate resolution in the mind, that as God calls, the world and all the concernments of it should be forsaken for Christ and the gospel. Our countenances and discourses in difficulties do not argue that this resolution is prevalent in us; but so it is required in that work of faith which we are in the consideration of.

2. A second thing that belongs hereunto is a peculiar remembrance of sin, and converse about it in our minds, with self-disciplinatory and abhorrence. God has promised in his covenant that he "will remember our sins no more," that is, to punish them; but it does not thence follow that we should no more remember them, to be humbled for them. Repentance respects sin always; wherever, therefore, that is, there will be a continual calling sin to remembrance. Says the psalmist, "My sin is ever before me." There is a threefold calling our past sins unto remembrance:—

(1.) With delight and contentment. Thus is it with profligate sinners, whose bodies are grown unserviceable unto their youthful lusts. They call over their former sins, roll them over in their minds, express their delight in them by their words, and have no greater trouble but that, for the want of strength or opportunity, they cannot still live in the practice of them: this is to be old in wickedness, and to have their bones filled with the sins of their youth. So do many in this age delight in filthy communication, unclean society, and all incentives of lust,—a fearful sign of being given over unto a reprobate mind, a heart that cannot repent.

(2.) There is a remembrance of sin unto disquietment, terror, and despair. Where men's consciences are not seared with a hot iron, sin will visit their minds ever and anon with a troublesome remembrance of itself, with its aggravating circumstances. For the most part men hide themselves from this visitor,—they are not at home, not at leisure to converse with it, but shift it off, like insolvent debtors, from day to day, with a few transient thoughts and words. But sometimes it will not be so put off,— it will come with an arrest or a warrant from the law of God, that shall make them stand and give an account of themselves. Hereon they are filled with disquietments, and some with horror and despair; which they seek to pacify and divert themselves from by further emerging [immersing?] themselves in the pursuit of their lusts. The case of Cain, Gen. iv. 13, 16, 17.

(3.) There is a calling former sins to remembrance as a furtherance of repentance; and so they are a threefold glass unto the souls wherein it has a treble object:—

[1.] It sees in them the depravation of its nature, the evil quality of that root which has brought forth such fruit; and they see in it their own folly, how they were cheated by sin and

Satan; they see the unthankfulness and unkindness towards God wherewith they were accompanied. This fills them with holy shame, Rom. vi. 21. This is useful and necessary unto repentance. Perhaps if men did more call over their former sins and miscarriages than they do, they would walk more humbly and warily than they do for the most part. So David in his age prays for a renewed sense of the pardon of the sins of his youth, Ps.xxv. 7.

[2.] The soul sees in them a representation of the grace, patience, and pardoning mercy of God. "Thus and thus was it with me: God might justly have cast me off for ever; he might have cut me off in the midst of these sins, so as that I should have had no leisure to have cried for mercy; and perhaps some of them were sins long continued in the infinite patience of God, that spared me! The infinite grace and mercy of God, that forgave unto me these provoking iniquities!" This frame is expressed, Ps. ciii. 3,4.

[3.] The soul sees herein the efficacy of the mediation and blood of Christ, 1 John ii. 2. "Whence is it that I have deliverance from the guilt of these sins that way was made for the advancing of grace in the pardon of them? Whence is it that my soul and conscience are purged from the stain and filth of them?" Here the whole glory of the love and grace of Christ in his mediation, with the worth of the atonement that he made, and the ransom that he paid, with the efficacy of his blood to purge us from all our sins, is represented unto the mind of the believer. So "out of the eater comes forth meat;" and thereby a reconciliation is made between the deepest humiliation and a refreshing sense of the love of God and peace with him.

This, therefore, a soul which is engaged into the paths of repentance will constantly apply itself unto; and it is faith alone whereunto we are beholding for the views of these things in sin. In no other light will they be seen therein. Their aspect in any other is horrid and terrifying, suited only to fill the soul with dread and horror, and thoughts of fleeing from God. But this view of them is suited to stir up all graces unto a holy exercise.

3. Hereon godly sorrow will ensue: this, indeed, is the very life and soul of repentance; so the apostle declares it, 2 Cor. vii. 9-11. And it comprises all that is spoken in the Scripture about a broken heart and a contrite spirit, which expresses itself by sighs, tears, mourning, yea, watering our beds with tears, and the like. David gives so great an instance in himself hereof, and that so frequently repeated, as that we need no other exemplification of it. I shall not at large insist upon it, but only show,—(1.) What it does respect; and, (2.) Wherein it does consist,—how faith works it in the soul.

(1) What it does respect; and it has a twofold object:—

[1.] Such past sins as, by reason of their own nature or their aggravations, have left the greatest impression on the conscience. It respects, indeed, in general, all past and known sins that can be called to remembrance; but usually, in the course of men's lives, there have been some sins whose wounds, on various accounts, have been most deep and sensible: these are the especial objects of this godly sorrow. So was it with David; in the whole course of his life, after his great fall, he still bewailed his miscarriage therein; the like respect he had unto the other sins of his youth. And none have been so preserved but they may fix on some such provocation as may be a just cause of this sorrow all their days.

[2.] It respects the daily incursions of infirmities, in failings, negligence in our frames or actions,—such as the best are subject to. These are a matter of continual sorrow and mourning to a gracious soul that is engaged in this duty and way of repentance.

(2.) Wherein it does consist; and the things following do concur therein:—

[1.] Self judging. This is the ground and spring of all godly sorrow, and thereon of repentance, turning away the displeasure of God, 1 Cor. xi. 31. This the soul does continually with reference unto the sins mentioned; it passes sentence on itself every day. This cannot be done without grief and sorrow; for although the soul finds it a necessary duty, and is thereon well pleased with it, yet all such self-reflections are like afflictions, not joyous, but grievous.

[2.] The immediate effect hereof is constant humiliation. He that so judges himself knows what frame of mind and spirit becomes him thereon. This takes away the ground from all pride, elation of mind, self-pleasing: where this self-judging is constant they can have no place. This is that frame of mind which God approves so highly, and has made such promises unto; the humble are everywhere proposed as the especial object of his own care; his respect is to them that are of a broken heart, and of a contrite spirit: and this will grow on no other root. No man, by his utmost diligence, on any argument or consideration, shall be able to bring himself into that humble frame wherein God is delighted, unless he lay the foundation of it in continual self-judging on the account of former and present sins. Men may put on a fashion, frame, and garb of humility; but really humble they are not. Where this is wanting, pride is in the throne, in the heart, though humility be in the countenance and deportment. And herein does this godly sorrow much consist.

[3.] There is in it a real trouble and disquietment of mind: for sorrow is an afflictive passion; it is contrary to that composure which the mind would constantly be at. Howbeit, this trouble is not such as is opposed unto spiritual peace and refreshment; for it is an effect of faith, and faith will produce nothing that is really inconsistent with peace with God, or that shall impeach it: but it is opposite unto other comforts. It is a trouble that all earthly things cannot take off and remove. This trouble of his mind, in his sorrow for sin, David on all occasions expresses unto God; and sometimes it rises to a great and dreadful height, as it is expressed, Ps.lxxxviii, throughout. Hereby the soul is sometimes overwhelmed; yet so as to relieve itself by pouring out its complaint before the Lord, Ps. cii. 1.

[4.] This inward frame of trouble, mourning, and contriteness, will express itself on all just occasions by the outward signs of sighs, tears , and mournful complaints. Ps. xxxi. 10. So David continually mentions his tears on the like account; and Peter, on the review of his sins wept bitterly; Mary washed the feet of Christ with her tears;—as we should all do. A soul filled with sorrow will run over and express its inward frame by these outward signs. I speak not of those self-whole, jolly professors which these days abound with; but such as faith engages in this duty will on all occasions abound in these things. I fear there is amongst us too great a pretence that men's natural tempers and constitutions are uncompliant with these things. Where God makes the heart soft, and godly sorrow does not only sometimes visit it, but dwell in it, it will not be wholly wanting in these expressions of it; and what it comes short of one way it may make up in another. Whatever the case be as to tears, it is certain that to multiply sighs and groans for sin is contrary to no man's constitution, but only to sin ingrafted in his constitution.

[5.] This godly sorrow will constantly incite the mind unto all duties, acts, and fruits of repentance whatever; it is never barren nor heartless, but being both a grace and a duty, it will stir up the soul unto the exercise of all graces, and the performance of all duties that are of the same kind. This the apostle declares fully, 2 Cor. vii.11. This, therefore, is another thing which belongs unto that state of repentance which faith will bring the soul unto, and whereby it will evidence itself on the occasions before mentioned; and indeed, if this sorrow be constant and operative, there is no clearer evidence in us of saving faith. They are blessed who thus mourn. I had almost said, it is worth all other evidences, as that without which they are none at all; where this frame is not in some good measure, the soul can have no pregnant evidence of its good estate.

4. Another thing that belongs to this state, is outward observances becoming it; such as abstinence, unto the due mortification of the flesh,—not in such things or ways as are hurtful unto nature, and really obstructive of greater duties. There have been great mistakes in this matter; most men have fallen into extremes about it, as is usual with the most in like cases. They did retain in the Papacy, from the beginning of the

apostasy of the church from the rule of the
Scripture, an opinion of the necessity of
mortification unto a penitent state; but they
mistook the nature of it, and placed it for the
most part in that which the apostle calls the
"doctrine of devils," when he foretold believers
of that hypocritical apostasy, 1 Tim. iv. 1-3.
Forbidding to marry, engaging one sort of men
by vows against the use of that ordinance of God
for all men, and enjoining abstinence from meats
in various laws and rules, under pretence of great
austerity, was the substance of their mortification.
Hereunto they added habits, fasting disciplines,
rough garments, and the like pretended self-
macerations innumerable. But the vanity of
this hypocrisy has been long since detected.
But therewithal most men are fallen into
the other extreme. Men do generally judge that
they are at their full liberty in and for the use of
the things esteemed refreshments of nature; yea,
they judge themselves not to be obliged unto any
retrenchment in garments, diet, with the free use
of all things in themselves lawful, when they are
under the greatest necessity of godly sorrow and
express repentance. But there is here a no less
pernicious mistake than in the former excess; and
it is that which our Lord Jesus Christ gives us in
charge to watch against, Luke xxi. 34-36. This,
therefore, I say, is required unto the state we
inquire after: those things which restrain the
satisfaction of the appetite, with an aversation of
the joyous enticements of the world, walking

heavily and mournfully, expressing an humble and afflicted frame of spirit, are necessary in such a season. The mourners in Zion are not to be ashamed of their lot and state, but to profess it in all suitable outward demonstration of it;—not in fantastical habits and gestures, like sundry orders of the monks; not in affected forms of speech, and uncouth deportments, like some among ourselves; but in such ways as naturally express the inward frame of mind inquired after.

5. There is required hereunto a firm watch over solitudes and retirements of the night and day, with a continual readiness to conflict temptations in their first appearance, that the soul be not surprised by them. The great design, in the exercise of this grace, is to keep and preserve the soul constantly in an humble and contrite frame; if that be lost at any time, the whole design is for that season disappointed. Wherefore, faith engages the mind to watch against two things:—

(1.) The times wherein we may lose this frame;
(2.) The means whereby. And,—

(1.) For the times. There are none to be so diligently watched over as our solitudes and retirements by night or by day. What we are in them, that we are indeed, and no more. They are either the best or the worst of our times, wherein the principle that is predominant in us will show and act itself. Hence some are said "to devise evil on their beds, and when the morning is light they practice it," Mic.ii. 1. Their solitude in the night serves them to think on, contrive, and delight in, all that iniquity which they intend by day to practice, according to their power. And on the other side, the work of a gracious soul in such seasons is to be seeking after Christ, Cant. iii. 1,—to be meditating of God, as the psalmist often expresses it. This, therefore, the humble soul is diligently watchful in, that at such seasons vain imaginations, which are apt to obtrude themselves on the mind, do not carry it away, and cause it to lose its frame, though but for a season; yea, these are the times which it principally lays hold on for its improvement: then does it call over all those considerations of sin and grace, which are meet to affect it and abase it.

(2.) For the means of the loss of an humble frame. They are temptations; these labour to possess the mind either by sudden surprisals or continued solicitations. A soul engaged by faith in this duty is aware always of their deceit and violence; it knows that if they enter into it, and do entangle it, though but for a season, they will quite cast out or deface that humble, contrite, broken frame, which it is its duty to preserve. And there is none who has the least grain of spiritual wisdom, but may understand of what sort these temptations are which he is obnoxious unto. Here, then, faith sets the soul on its watch and guard continually, and makes it ready to combat every temptation on its first appearance, for then it is weakest and most easily to be subdued; it will suffer them to get neither time, nor ground, nor strength: so it preserves an humble frame,—delivers it frequently from the jaws of this devourer.

6. Although the soul finds satisfaction in this condition, though it be never sinfully weary of it, nor impatient under it, yea, though it labour to grow and thrive in the spirit and power of it, yet it is constantly accompanied with deep sighs and groanings for its deliverance. And these groanings respect both what it would be delivered from and what it would attain unto; between which there is an interposition of some sighs and groans of nature, for a continuance in its present state.

(1.) That which this groaning respects deliverance from is the remaining power of sin; this is that which gives the soul its distress and disquietment. Occasionally, indeed, its humility, mourning, and self-abasement are increased by it; but this is through the efficacy of the grace of Christ Jesus,—in its own nature it tends to hurt and ruin. This the apostle emphatically expresses in his own person, as bearing the place and state of other believers, Rom. vii. 24.

And this constant groaning for deliverance from the power of sin excites the soul to pursue it unto its destruction. No effect of faith, such as this is, is heartless or fruitless; it will be operative towards what it aims at,—and that in this case is the not-being of sin: this the soul groans after, and therefore contends for. This is the work of faith, and "faith without works is dead:" wherefore it will continually pursue sin unto all its retirements and reserves. As it can have no rest from it, so it will give neither rest nor peace unto it; yea, a constant design after the not-being of sin, is a blessed evidence of a saving faith.

(2.) That which it looks after is the full enjoyment of glory, Rom. viii. 23. This, indeed, is the grace and duty of all believers, of all who have received the first-fruits of the Spirit; they all in their measure groan that their very bodies may be delivered from being the subject and seat of sin,—that they may be redeemed out of that bondage. It is a bondage to the very body of a believer, to be instrumental unto sin. This we long for its perfect deliverance from, which shall complete the grace of adoption in the whole person. But it is most eminent in those who excel in a state of humiliation and repentance. They, if any, groan earnestly,—this they sigh, breathe, and pant after continually; and their views of the glory that shall be revealed give them refreshment in their deepest sorrows; they wait for the Lord herein more than they that wait for the morning. Do not blame a truly penitent soul if he longs to be dissolved; the greatness and excellency of the change which he shall have thereby is his present life and relief.

(3.) But there is a weight on this desire, by the interposition of nature for the continuation of its present being, which is inseparable from it. But faith makes a reconciliation of these repugnant inclinations, keeping the soul from weariness and impatience. And this it does by reducing the mind unto its proper rock: it lets it know that it ought not absolutely to be under the conduct of either of these desires. First, it keeps them from excess, by teaching the soul to regulate them both by the word of God: this it makes the rule of such desires and inclinations; which whilst they are regulated by, we shall not offend in them. And it mixes a grace with them both that makes them useful,— namely, constant submission to the will of God. "This grace would have, and this nature would have; but," says the soul, "the will and sovereign pleasure of God is my rule: "Not my will, holy Father, but thy will be done." We have the example of Christ himself in this matter.

7. The last thing I shall mention, as that which completes the state described, is abounding in contemplations of things heavenly, invisible, and eternal. None have more holy and humble thoughts than truly penitent souls, none more high and heavenly contemplations. You would take them to be all sighs, all mourning, all dejection of spirit; but none are more above,— none more near the high and lofty One. As he dwells with them, Isa. lvii. 15, so they dwell with him in a peculiar manner, by these heavenly contemplations. Those who have lowest thoughts of themselves, and are most filled with self-

abasement, have the clearest views of divine glory. The bottom of a pit or well gives the best prospect of the heavenly luminaries; and the soul in its deepest humiliations has for the most part the clearest views of things within the veil.

Printed in the United States
149369LV00001B/126/A